Dancing With The Doorknob

or

The other day as I was falling off my bicycle ...

by Charlie O'Dowd

Tangential Press
Boulder, Colorado

Published by Tangential Press, an imprint of Luminous Moon Press,
Boulder, CO. luminousmoon.com

First Edition: June 2025

ISBN-13: 979-8-9916548-9-0

Humor & Entertainment / Television — Humor Essays — Biography
& Autobiography / Memoirs — Biography & Autobiography / People
with Disabilities — Biography & Autobiography / Entertainment &
Performing Arts — Performing Arts / Television — Performing Arts /
Film — Performing Arts / Theater

Printed and bound in the United States of America

Advance Praise for
Dancing With The Doorknob

Bob Odenkirk – American actor, screenwriter, comedian, and producer, *Better Call Saul* and *Breaking Bad*

Charlie has a unique story and the best energy – his personal strength and good nature have led him forward through tough stuff. I am thankful for the energy I got from reading his story!

* * *

Victoria Principal – American actress, producer, author, and entrepreneur

I think you are bringing a very important subject to the public. Your kind and compassionate nature infuses your story and elevates your experiences in a way that makes the reader feel included in even the most intimate moments.

Thank you for reaching out to so many others, especially veterans.

* * *

Stew Lyons – PGA, Producer *Breaking Bad, Better Call Saul*

A personal and deeply felt account of what it means to be truly "behind the scenes" and helping make it all happen.

* * *

Dr. Douglas Meintz, DC, BCN

Dancing With The Doorknob *could easily be described as a cross between a weight loss guide (because there were times when I laughed my ass off) and a handbook on persistence, resilience and rugged determination.*

Charlie's ability to view the ups and downs of life, the moments that go sideways and the people who helped him along the way is magical. He writes in a way that inspires hope, promotes healing and illustrates the power of gratitude.

My wish is that this book finds its way into the hands of all who aspire to make the most of their lives, their relationships and their impact on their communities.

* * *

Randy McComas – Videographer, editor, best friend

A very unique way to tell a story. Your story – a great way to de-brief your life dealing with TBI and have a blast doing it.

* * *

Ann Lerner – Producer, Albuquerque Film Commissioner

You hid your challenges well. We had no clue what you were going through.

Table of Contents

Mickey Rourke – YIKES ! • Cheyney State • Fight Night – Sports TV • Public Safety Ad – Like A Blue Movie • Super Bowl Commercials – Sierra Mist & Coke

Foreword

D*ancing With The Doorknob* is a recounting of my struggle with a traumatic brain injury (TBI) while enjoying rewarding careers as a film producer and college professor. The bulk of the chapters are stories from film and TV sets, from *City Slickers* to *Breaking Bad*, with occasional asides to personal shenanigans : 80% stories from sets, 10% medical challenges, and 10% family anecdotes. Like *People* magazine in a book.

Inspiration

L ife has been a continual adventure. Many friends over the years have remarked at the unusual experiences in my life, saying that I should write a book. So here we are.

I was inspired by three books I'd read recently: *Bossypants* by Tina Fey, *Rough Draft* by Katy Tur, and *The Good Neighbor: The Life and Work of Fred Rogers* by Maxwell King.

All three interweave experiences in TV and film production with moments in their personal lives – some comic, some not so much. The same is true here. Personal stories from film and TV sets sprinkled with family anecdotes, both happy and tragic.

Lucky for me, I chose to be a clown and work in entertainment. It saved my life. Spending countless hours on sets with 50 of my closest friends, weaving stories into feature films and TV productions, a camaraderie like no other. I credit the industry for what little stability I was clinging to.

Lastly, I have to credit Walter Matthau for my subtitle. In 1967 he won the Best Supporting Actor Oscar for his role in *The Fortune Cookie*. He strode to the stage with a cast on his arm and turned to reveal numerous cuts and bruises on his face. He started his acceptance speech with : *"The other day as I was falling off my bicycle …."* Rowdy applause ended his sentence mid-stride.

Thanks, Walter.

 See Walter's acceptance speech on YouTube at : https://www.youtube.com/watch?v=K1-q8YzxEys. Go to 1:15 in the clip for his speech.

Introduction

L ife is good. I've had more Golden Moments than I could have imagined, and I'm grateful ... but ...

In 1983, I was 32 and rocketing towards my goal as an entertainer, destined for Broadway and feature films. I recently graduated from the University of New Mexico (UNM) with a theater degree and experience as an actor and director. I had the goods.

That summer, I co-directed *The Sound Of Music* and played lead actor in the hit musical *Stop The World – I Want to Get Off*. The productions were a big deal, staged in Albuquerque's Popejoy Hall, a 2,000 seat theater, and selling 1,500 tickets each night.

15,000 people saw me sing in *Stop the World,* rewarding our cast with standing ovations every night. The local press sang my praises. Next step was auditioning on Broadway. My mentor, a Broadway and broadcast TV veteran, told me I was ready.

To infinity and beyond !

As if that all wasn't enough, during the show I fell in love with Johanna Johnson, a dream come true. We moved in together right away. The world was my oyster. I just starred in a great play, had a theater degree in my back pocket AND was newly in love. Young, handsome, talented – opportunity was glowing like the morning sun.

Then I broke my head.

It was just a few weeks after the play closed and I'd returned to a job as counselor at the Children's Psychiatric Center. Heading home at 11 PM, I crashed my bike and slid down the road on my face, resulting in 40 stitches at the hairline above my right eye and more to my face. Devastating injuries.

One of the docs in the ER had front-line experience in a combat M.A.S.H. unit and sewed my head tight. I remember spending weeks on the couch recuperating with Johanna's loving attention.

But there was no medical follow-up, no referral to a Neurologist or any specialist to guide me through recovery. I don't remember anything from the following year, other than a couple of inactive months.

I remember that, more than a year later, I had no sense of balance, consistently drifting to my right as I walked, smashing into door jams when I simply tried to walk through. I had to give up tennis and basketball.

During that year, Johanna and I were married and moved from New Mexico to the DC area. I'll explain later why that mattered. We chose DC to be near family. I intended to take the train to NY to audition for Broadway shows.

But, where to start ? Shortly before moving, I read about the new director of The American National Theater at the Kennedy Center. Peter Sellers (not the famed actor) was 26 years old and I wanted to work with him. I was less than a year out of college and any professional experience would be a plus. Starting at a prestigious venue like the Kennedy Center fit my personality, a tendency to meet any challenge with guns blazing. Nothing could stop me now – or so I thought.

I made the first move, driving to the Kennedy Center and marching in with head held high. But I stalled. I stood outside Seller's office suite for a long time, frozen, unable to step in and ask for a job. My courage was gone. Up until that point in my life I had always taken charge – blasting through hurdles to reach my goals. Somehow, I couldn't stand up for myself.

With my tail between my legs, I slinked home.

Smarting from that failure I looked for any opportunity. I auditioned and was cast in a dinner theater production in the DC suburbs, playing Pawnee Bill in *Annie Get Your Gun*. It was the last time I performed, 1984.

The owners of the dinner theater were kind. They recognized my maturity and asked me to manage the place, which was good because my first son was on his way and we lacked health insurance. I was glad to get full-time work, but they insisted that I run the place and not act in any shows. Again, I slinked away with my tail safely tucked away. I lacked the courage to pursue my goal of performing.

Mental confusion hung over me like a cloud, blocking the sun and chilling my confidence. And there were plenty of drugs and alcohol to cover my discomfort and disappointments. I lived in a fog, usually intoxicated when not working. I knew that it wasn't good for me, but it was a condition that I understood, void of confusion because that voice had been muted. I had no idea that my change in personality was related to the head injury.

After nearly 40 years, in 2020, I sought help from neurologists. They confirmed that the effects of the injury were clear and would continue to challenge me. I had heard of TBI, traumatic brain injury, related to the NFL and the military but hadn't linked the head injury to my daily struggles. The fog started to clear.

* * *

I don't want sympathy, I want to understand and to raise awareness. Our collective understanding of brain injuries is lacking. Every therapist I've encountered has lumped brain injuries in with general trauma – not true, it's different. And health insurance is unwilling to pay for appropriate care.

Traumatic brain injuries and lack of social integration have both been shown to increase risk for suicidal ideation and suicide attempts. Studies have linked traumatic brain injury (TBI) and post-traumatic stress disorder (PTSD) to suicide in military veterans. A 2019 study found that veterans with a history of TBI are more than twice as likely to die by suicide than those without a TBI diagnosis. An average of 22 veterans kill themselves every day, an epidemic devastating countless families.

I became aware of the lasting effects of my injury while interviewing an Army Vet challenged with a TBI. He spoke of isolation and fear and I saw myself in his statements. More on that in the chapter "Sky Warriors".

I'm an old hippie. My injury was from rank stupidity, riding a bicycle without a helmet. No need to feel sorry for me. But many TBI survivors suffered their injuries in the military, defending our freedoms. They deserve better support.

I've had difficulty finding services. But I'm a senior blessed with a supportive family and lots of friends. I WILL find help. I can't imagine what life's choices are like for a Veteran living on the streets with scant resources, struggling with a broken brain. The same for NFL players who suffered repeated concussions for our enjoyment on Sunday.

I'm hoping to bring some level of understanding to the general public about this invisible disability.

* * *

It's 2024 and I live near DC again with my son and grandson.

Yesterday I contracted with a new primary physician. Relating my health history I mentioned the TBI. I was surprised to hear that she had a history with patients struggling with TBI and CTE. CTE, Chronic Traumatic Encephalopathy, is a progressive and fatal brain disease that can develop in people who have experienced repeated concussions or other traumatic brain injuries. She related that one of her clients had committed suicide in frustration. The same fate has plagued NFL veterans after repeated concussions.

In 2000, Doctors with the NFL raised the issue due to lingering effects on the mental health of league veterans. Boston University found Chronic Traumatic Encephalopathy in the brains of 345 out of 376 players, or 92% of former NFL players studied.

92% ! YIKES ! Who was your favorite lineman ?

When I shared that the TBI diagnosis and related therapies had only begun four years previous, she asked the question I've been asking myself for years : "Why didn't anyone notice that I was struggling after the injury and suggest getting help ?"

The answer lies in the move to DC. In Albuquerque, I was a fixture in the theater community. Everybody knew me and expected much. In DC no one knew me. There were no expectations. And with a child on the way, I accepted a new reality, dad. I was busy enough to not notice the change.

Looking back, I'm amazed that no one noticed or spoke up, including myself. The personality change had been drastic. In just a few short weeks, I transitioned from a "type A" personality ready to belt a tune to a thousand fans to a frightened little boy, unable to sing if anyone was listening. From leading man to house manager in just a few weeks.

The confusion ruled my world for the next 35 years yet I thrived in two professional careers : first as a filmmaker on feature films like *Young Guns II* and *City Slickers* and on hit TV shows, ending with two seasons on *Breaking Bad* and three more on *Better Call Saul*. I also taught film production in college for fifteen years at UNM and CNM, Central New Mexico Community College.

The bottom line is life and work have been a ball of fun – too many good times with celebrities and interesting projects to complain about it now. I could have gone further sans injury. I could have completed the journey, directing big-ticket feature films and belting favorite hits on Broadway stages to standing ovations.

But that's not the purpose of remembering the details here. After two days of neurological testing back in Albuquerque Dr. Pendleton remarked that, based on the data from the testing, he was surprised that I had functioned professionally. He spoke of Neuroplasticity, the ability of neural networks in the brain to change through growth and reorganization. It's when the brain is rewired to function in some way that differs from how it previously functioned. In layman's terms, the undamaged sections of the brain somehow reach across to the damaged areas and help them function.

So, there it is. My life's been a roller coaster of successes and disappointments with much to be celebrated. I'm happy.

Living A Dream

When I enrolled in college at the University of New Mexico I had one hope – to be a film director. But the lone film teacher was a whack job and the TV teacher was an alcoholic, so I tried my hand in the Theater Arts program.

Over the next three years, I studied under and assisted Dr. Bob Hartung who had excelled in the early days of broadcast TV. Bob was floor director on *The Sid Caesar Hour* and wrote numerous teleplay adaptations for the original Hallmark Hall of Fame, earning nominations for prime-time Emmy Awards for his teleplays for *Inherit The Wind, The Magnificent Yankee,* and *The Patriots.*

Bob supported my desire to direct but insisted that I expand my reach, casting me in plays that he directed. The experience was thrilling and my dream grew to visions of acting on Broadway.

Original Monkey Boy : I was a born filmmaker. Here I am at 3 years old re-enacting the monkey scene from the beginning of 2001 : A Space Odyssey.

Under his direction I sang, danced and acted my heart out, discovering talents that I didn't know I had. He cast me in *The Unknown Soldier and His Wife*, an anti-war comedy written by Peter Ustinov. I played the Archbishop, the role that Ustinov wrote for himself.

Shortly after graduation, I was cast as the lead in Anthony Newley's musical *Stop The World – I Want To Get Off* staged in Albuquerque's Popejoy Hall, a 2,000 seat theater built to host the Symphony and traveling Broadway shows. We sold 1,500 seats each night for ten shows – 15,000 guests saw the show and rewarded us with standing ovations every night.

When the show wrapped, I sought advice from Dr. Bob. He was very supportive, having seen the show twice. He knew that I had hopes of acting on Broadway, so I was thrilled when he told me that I was ready to chase that dream. He was realistic, stating that there were no guarantees but that I had the goods and should take my chances.

A month later I broke my head in a horrible bicycle accident requiring forty stitches at the hairline above my right eye. Overnight my personality changed from a leading man to a confused hermit, unable to sing to anyone but my wife.

I had suffered a TBI, a traumatic brain injury.

* * *

Playing Littlechap in *Stop The World* was my first step toward living the dream. Standing on stage night after night, bathed in applause for a job well done. It's thrilling to truly move an audience and humbling to stand for five minutes on stage while the audience rises in a sustained ovation. We sold fifteen hundred tickets a night – a standing ovation of that size is like an emotional tsunami for the performers – and they did it every night.

Stop The World was my fifth play, and the first since graduating from a college theater program. I'd acted in three plays directed by my mentor, Daddy Bob Hartung, all on UNM stages. *The Travelin' Show* and *The Unknown*

Soldier And His Wife were staged in Rodey Theater. Rodey has 440 seats with a professional fly system for scenery, and ample wings for entrances. *The History Of American Film* was staged in The X, UNM's Experimental Theatre, a black box with 120 seats, no fly system and no wings, a true fly-by-the-seat-of-your-pants experience.

Both Rodey and The X were nestled in the theater department, surrounded by a costume shop, a scene-building shop, dressing rooms, and a green room, very cozy and protected. *Stop The World* was staged by ACLOA, The Albuquerque Civic Light Opera Association in Popejoy Hall – a 2,000 seat house built for Broadway road shows, plus symphony and dance concerts. Popejoy Hall and Rodey Theater were housed in UNM's Fine Arts building along with a music department and Fine Arts Museum.

Audiences entered both Popejoy Hall and Rodey Theater from the Fine Arts Lobby. They were a mere sixty feet apart. But the experience in Popejoy was a different world, in the same building but separate from the safety of the college program. Sink or Swim.

The experience started with work on *The Sound Of Music*. That Summer, my buddy, Fred Maio, had been hired by ACLOA to direct and he asked me to join him and direct the kids, the Von Trappe kids. Fred and I bonded and we co-directed the production.

Even though we were working in a community theater production we were on a professional stage. The experience was a huge step up.

Breaking Bad and *Better Call Saul*

Never Shake A Baby

In 2008 the economy was in the dumps and the stress on families was intense, leading to a rise in domestic violence. My neighbor was the head of Pediatrics at University Hospital and she was concerned. She said that the incidence of "shaken baby syndrome" was reaching an epidemic level. She asked if it was possible to produce a public service announcement (PSA) to run on local TV, alerting the public to the danger.

I wrote a 30-second story featuring a frustrated dad struggling with a crying infant. The message would be spoken by a caring adult who magically appears to help. I went to the UNM Theater Dept. to cast the frustrated dad but hadn't cast the 'helper' yet.

I was strolling Albuquerque's trendy Nob Hill district one evening when I caught a glimpse of Bryan Cranston, recent star of *Malcolm in the Middle*. What were the odds ?

So I screwed up my courage and approached him. I told him about the doctor and the problem and he signed on without hesitation. He gave me contact info for his management to set up the deal.

I was teaching filmmaking both at UNM and CNM at the time and looked for worthwhile projects for the students to shoot. Here was a chance to shoot a PSA for an issue that matters with a bonafide Hollywood star. Rock and roll ! We shot at my house with 30 students and all the equipment needed from the schools.

Bryan arrived on a motor scooter to the students delight. I'd hired four friends from the industry to guide the students, creating a workshop with teachers in camera, grip/electric, makeup and the art department. I served as producer/director. Bryan was supportive of film education and was very gracious with the students.

 You can see the PSA on YouTube at : https://www.youtube.com/ watch?v=JS8b6ajge-Y&t=52s

Breaking Bad

Luck had it that great weather, generous tax incentives, direct flights and top notch crews drew much of Hollywood to New Mexico. When I started in the biz in '87 we were lucky to get any feature films at all. We survived on commercials and music videos.

But that all changed in 2007 when some Angels from LA invested $97 million bucks to build a state of the art production facility with sound stages south of Albuquerque. The stages attracted big time features and TV productions like *Breaking Bad, The Book of Eli,* and *Independence Day: Resurgence.* That started a snowball rolling downhill.

Producers planning to shoot in any town get the crew lists from the last couple of productions and start there to hire their crew. Word got out that the crews in New Mexico were second to none. The snowball got bigger.

I was producing and directing EPK segments for the many TV shows and features shooting all over the state. EPK, Electronic Press Kit, videos of the crew behind the scenes. Plus interviews with the cast and directors to be used in future marketing of the show.

Then I got the "Golden Ticket" !

I was asked to run an EPK crew in the fourth season of *Breaking Bad.* I proclaim this as a Golden Ticket moment due to the kindness, humanity and clear vision of the writers, actors, and crew on that show. The vast majority of experiences on set and with stars had been quite positive, but this was different.

There was a cohesion, a shared purpose that resonated from the top throughout the cast and crew. Starting with Vince Gilligan and exec producers Melissa Bernstein and Michelle McClaren, through Bryan Cranston and the dedicated cast. It was a joy to come to work. Even fifteen hour days were a pleasure.

I can't move on without mentioning Stew Lyons, a producer with a calm control and heart of gold. Stew was always looking out for his crew. What's the next step in their career and how can he help. Over the many seasons Stew promoted crew members up the ladder, from Production Managers and First AD's to Associate Producers.

In 2013 the show received the Best Dramatic Series Emmy. The producers, writers and cast joined Vince on stage to accept the award. All but the writers had to catch a red eye to be back on set the next morning in Albuquerque.

In the office, I congratulated Stew on the win. He motioned for me to wait a moment while he stepped into his office. He returned and handed me the Emmy statue, declaring that the entire production team won the award. He had a staff member snap a photo of us together with me holding the Emmy, a great honor !

Me with Stew Lyons and The Emmy.

* * *

The level of professionalism from the film crew was above and beyond. Every department head was the best I'd ever worked with, from makeup to wardrobe to props, the best.

Often there are magical moments on set that make the whole enterprise special. Towards the end of the series Walter White kidnaps his infant child, Holly, and drives off, with his wife, Skyler, running after him in tears.

Any fan of the show would realize that Walter will have a second thought, realizing that he had to return the baby. The writers crafted a scene in a gas station bathroom where Walt changes Holly's diaper. There's no dialogue but you can 'see' the wheels turning in his head.

The construction crew built the bathroom on stage in a hurry, the baseboard paint was still drying as the camera rolled. The crew gathered near the camera as Walt exited the bathroom, holding Holly. Suddenly, this one year old started calling for "mommy" in her sweet, tiny voice. We were stunned, covering our mouths to muffle our surprise. How can an infant understand the complexity of her situation ?

* * *

On every production the crew sign NDA's, Non Disclosure Agreements. It's standard practice. You have to protect the show's secrets until it airs.

At the final wrap party I invited my son, Keaton, as my plus one. He had to sign an NDA to attend. The party was fantastic ! Vince and the cast made heartfelt speeches while we wined and dined. When I introduced Keaton to a crew member from the FX team he whipped out his phone and asked him "do you want to see something cool" ?

He proceeded to show a video he'd shot of the M60 machine gun in the trunk of the Caddy that kills Jack's hoodlum crew in the final episode. Holy Shit ! Keaton was 22 but I questioned whether he could keep the secret. He did. Now a Staff Sergeant in the Marines, he just told me that he signs NDA's all the time and the consequences for a slip with military intelligence are far greater than what Hollywood could ever prescribe.

* * *

The transition from *Breaking Bad* to *Better Call Saul* was smooth for the New Mexico crew. Although *Saul* was a different show, there were cast crossovers making it seem like the same show with different sets. The majority of the crew continued onto *Saul*.

Jonathan Banks, Giancaro Esposito and Bob Odenkirk returned and were joined by fresh characters played by Rhea Seehorn, Michael McKean, Patrick Fabian, and Michael Mando. All great talents, all humble and kind.

Keaton, Bryan Cranston, and me at <u>Breaking Bad</u> final wrap party.

Bryan Cranston

What can you say about Bryan Cranston ? From playing the dad on *Malcolm in the Middle* to the dentist on *Seinfeld* and, finally, to Walter White, Bryan has a range of believability that stretches across genres. You believe him when he's a fumbling oaf, creating mayhem with his kids, and you believe him when he stares down drug kingpins.

Watching him create on set was very entertaining but chatting with him face-to-face was special. I got to interview him at least 25 times over two seasons. Bryan was open about his role and often resorted to improv in character during interviews.

For the actors, stepping aside for interviews can break their concentration, slipping from character to real life, but Bryan cruised through with humor, thrilled with his place in this circus. In the fifth season AMC decided to create a short video to follow each episode, with background footage and interviews explaining the issues central to shooting the pivotal scenes in that episode. I was hired to direct.

Each five minute clip played on AMC online following the episode. You can see the 16 short films chronicling the final season on YouTube.

Search for videos on YouTube at : *Making of Breaking Bad Episode 501* (through episode 516)

* * *

Each interview was a chance for Bryan to cascade into a stand-up routine for me and my crew. In the interview on episode 501 he points out a huge magnet that they get from a junk yard. Bryan dryly explains that it's a B.A.M., a big ass magnet. He says it's an industry term. What ?

It was hard to keep a straight face, especially when I sat him together with Aaron Paul. They played off each other like a seasoned comedy team. Their energy was contagious.

Then, in an instant, he was Walter White again as the AD calls for him on set.

There was a marked difference in his demeanor during filming of the show's final episode. The company was set to film the scenes where Walt confronts his partners from college, recruiting them for his plan to enrich his kids while threatening to have them shot. It may have been the gravity of the scene at hand or the fact that his run on the show was ending after five wonderful years but he was not as playful as usual, matter of fact in our interview, and he sat to himself, reading the paper between takes.

* * *

My favorite memory of Bryan is from the day we shot the PSA *Never Shake A Baby.* He was sitting on a couch in my family room between setups with students from UNM and CNM.

At one point I noticed him focus on a painting on the wall. It's a self portrait that my grandfather painted many decades past. The moment just felt special.

I highly recommend Bryan's autobiography entitled *A Life In Parts.*

Breaking Bad and Albuquerque

Breaking Bad was an international hit, with tourists traveling from Europe to visit filming locations from the show. Some came just to throw a pizza on the roof of Walter White's house, mimicking a scene from the show. A clerk at my local grocery store in Virginia Beach is flying to Albuquerque with his family to take the tour this month. The final episode of the show aired in 2013, eleven years ago.

For the City of Albuquerque it became an identifier. Like the arch to St. Louis or the bridge to San Francisco. For locals, we were living in the middle of it – in the middle of the fictional *Breaking Bad* world.

Walter White's house is in the Northeast Heights. Jesse lived in the opulent Country Club area. And the dilapidated industrial area, the rail yards, is only blocks South of downtown. The gas station where Walter White blows up a new Beemer is on Lomas Blvd, 10 minutes from my house. The Denny's where he eats breakfast on his 52nd birthday and inspects the machine gun in his trunk was on Central Ave. across from the University, UNM. We lived in the *Breaking Bad* world.

Location Managers on films and TV shows have to guide the company to each location. Maps are distributed on set and signs are posted on roadways to guide the crew. But, since signs could attract unwelcome visitors, they're written in code. For the last season of *Breaking Bad* the signs read 'WW'.

A benefit of working in film and TV is the myriad of locations where you spend your work days. The final season of *Breaking Bad* had great locations ; shooting in an active junkyard in hard hats and safety vests, on the banks of the Rio Grande in a cottonwood forest, on the red dirt of the Navajo Nation West of town – the variety adds to the experience, with new challenges every day.

In the cottonwood forest, production added a snake wrangler to protect us from varmints. It's standard practice. Any crew member can call for the wrangler rather than risk corralling a snake by themselves. And that leads to a second danger, getting stuck talking to a snake wrangler.

Finally, Jack's compound, where Jesse is held captive to cook for Todd, was a great find. Christian, the Location Manager, found it on Google Maps. The size of the industrial lot, with large machinery and outbuildings, drew him to scout the site. It was abandoned and slated for demolition. That means the landowner is motivated to take a fee and let you film to your hearts delight. Free money. Film companies come with cash and are heavily insured.

There were three great 'film sets' in the compound; the underground bunker where Jesse is held captive, the quonset hut where Jesse cooks, and Uncle Jack's clubhouse, where the entire gang meets their demise.

The quonset hut played as a full interior, with a full meth lab, where Walt dies. But the bunker and the clubhouse were filmed as exteriors then re-created on stage at the Albuquerque Studios to shoot interiors.

The death scene in the clubhouse was shot onstage. There's a five minute 'behind the scenes' video of the scene where you see the wiring that fires the squibs masquerading as bullet hits as the gang members fall dead like so many bowling pins.

 Watch *Making of Breaking Bad, Episode 516*

I wonder what's built on the property now.

Bob Odenkirk – *Better Call Saul*

On *Breaking Bad* I had the privilege of interviewing the cast, including Bob Odenkirk. Bob was squirrelly. He seemed a bit out of place amongst the serious, dramatic actors. He was always very professional when the camera was rolling, but in downtime he seemed to revert to his comic persona. Bob had been a writer on *Saturday Night Live* but he preferred the zany comedy of Monty Python. It was evident in his skits for the HBO hit *Mr. Show with Bob and David*.

Jump ahead to *Better Call Saul* and the tables had turned. Now he was the leading actor in a dramatic series, not what he'd been used to. On set he always looked serious. None of the flighty comic that I'd known on *Breaking Bad*. In an interview I asked him about the difference. He told me that his time on *Breaking Bad* had been a lark. He considered himself a supporting actor with little responsibility for the success of the show. But now he was the lead and it humbled him. He said that he realized that the success of the show was squarely on his shoulders. That the crew and the rest of the cast depended on him to perform. If the show tanked, all of these people would lose their jobs. He felt the weight of the responsibility. I already liked Bob but my respect for him tripled.

I'm currently reading Bob's book entitled *Comedy, Comedy, Comedy, Drama* in which he explores his career arc from standup comic to his stint on *Breaking Bad* and the lead role on *Better Call Saul*. I highly recommend the book. It's filled with his personal encounters in the biz with scores of comedians and gigs on shows from *The Ben Stiller Show* to *Arrested Development*, from improv at *Second City* to *Saturday Night Live* to *Mr. Show*.

At *Second City*, Bob wrote the famed character Matt Foley for Chris Farley featured on SNL. Matt Foley was the motivational speaker who "… lived in a van down by the river." It's one of my favorite SNL sketches.

* * *

While working on *Better Call Saul* I had a conversation with a makeup artist. She had worked with Vince Gilligan, the creator of *Breaking Bad*, and Bryan on *The X-Files*, season six, episode two entitled "Drive". Bryan played a somewhat repulsive character who takes Fox Mulder hostage.

During the shoot she had Bryan in the chair, working on his makeup, when Vince walked up. He said to Bryan "I'm gonna write a series and you're gonna star in it." After Vince walked away Bryan turned to the makeup gal and stated, dryly, "They all say that."

The rest is history !

Again, I recommend Bryan's memoir *A Life In Parts*. His life is as fascinating and complex as his characters.

* * *

My favorite sequence on *Better Call Saul* is the scene where Jimmy saves the worker dangerously hanging from the billboard. It's a perfect example of the complications involved in high ticket shots. Bob's character ping-pongs between his birth name, Jimmy McGill, and his contrived persona, Saul Goodman.

For those who haven't seen the show, the scene involves Jimmy hiring a worker to remove his billboard to avoid a lawsuit. It's all a scam, with Jimmy filming himself for the news, complaining that his brothers law firm, HHM was bullying him. But the worker falls off the scaffolding and dangles by his safety harness, fifty feet above the ground. Jimmy scurries up the ladder to save him. It's a hero shot for the news.

The scene was shot in the parking lot of Albuquerque High. The school was next to a busy freeway with the base of the roadway 40 feet higher than the parking lot. Hence, a billboard had been erected high enough to entice the passing highway traffic. Production rented the billboard and had an advertisement created and pasted on the frame. It featured Jimmy and was made to mimic ads for HHM.

The sign worker starts on the scaffolding, protected from a fall by a harness attached to the sign frame. What the viewer doesn't see is a massive construction crane high above the scene and out of frame, securing a safety line to the actor. The safety line would be "painted out," removed digitally, in post.

Jimmy addresses the camera with the billboard and worker in the background when the worker slips and falls off of the scaffold. The camera operator reacts, sending Jimmy scrambling to save the day.

He climbs onto the ladder and starts to climb. That's where they cut.

Production continued the next day on the backlot of the Q Studio stages. The producers had contracted for an exact replica of the billboard to be built just twelve feet above the ground to get all of the medium shots and closeups safely.

One shot had the camera on the scaffold, looking straight down as Jimmy climbs the ladder. It looks ominous, but it was only twelve feet off the ground with a large crash pad below Bob.

The crash pad was covered with a green screen so the editor could take this very safe moment and extend it to have Bob climbing 40 feet up the ladder for the show.

The *Saul* crew was very efficient. The departments worked seamlessly, always prepping for the next shot. So it was unusual to see the cast ready on set, the camera operator ready to pull the trigger, yet no call from the AD to stand by. Scanning the crew, I noticed that three producers were pacing with their cell phones pasted to their heads. They were talking to lawyers. Someone alerted the director that Bob would have to be in a safety harness to climb the ladder following OSHA rules, thus causing more work in post, painting out the harness and cables in each frame, and there are 24 frames per second.

I heard Stew Lyons argue that Bob would never be more than 12 feet off the ground with a large crash pad positioned below him for safety. He argued that the crash pad should negate the OSHA rule for a safety harness. Apparently the lawyers agreed and production pressed forward with only a twenty minute delay.

* * *

In numerous episodes, Jimmy hires a group of film students from the local college. That was fun for me since the local college was UNM, my Alma Mater, where I was a film and theater student 35 years before. Their equipment cases are stamped 'UNM'. The student director was played by a young actor named Josh Fadem. I recognized Josh for playing the fumbling pet talent agent with Tina Fey on *30 Rock*. Josh was thrilled that I recognized him and had enjoyed his performance. We had some laughs between takes.

* * *

Bob speaks of a personal moment in his book, both gratifying and humbling. He was entering a store on an LA street while a crane lifted the image of himself at the phone booth from *Better Call Saul* to the top of the building. It was a four story tall billboard of the show poster. That's something they do in LA, multi-story billboards to pitch the latest show. He said that it was as impressive as it was intimidating.

* * *

I last worked on *Better Call Saul* in the third season, before handing the gig to good friend Gary Marsh. By that time my crew and I had worked with the company for five seasons including the fourth and fifth seasons of *Breaking Bad*. We had free reign on the set and in the offices. There are often long breaks between camera set ups. We had the luxury of hanging out in whatever sets were standing by – Chuck McGil's house (Micheal McKean), or Kim Wexler's apartment. Fully dressed stage sets are fun to hang out on. The rest of the world only sees these sets on TV. We're hangin' out, drinking coffee and swapping war stories on a set where a major character gets whacked at the end of the show. A pretend world.

Jonathan Banks

Jonathan played Mike in *Better Call Saul* and *Breaking Bad*. The character, Mike, is a crusty old criminal with an understanding heart. He's inventive, shooting sneakers hanging on a wire to sprinkle cocaine on a rival's passing delivery truck. And he's brutal, from hand to hand takedowns to headshots, he always wins the day.

Back up to 1984 and *Beverly Hills Cop*. Jonathan's the henchman that kills Eddie Murphy's friend in Detroit. But Murphy returns the favor at the end of the film, blowing Jonathan away in a shootout. In an earlier encounter, Murphy confronts Jonathan's criminal boss in a private men's club. Jonathan tries to take charge, grabbing at Murphy. But Murphy responds, throwing him through the lavish buffet table. Jonathan rolls across the table through the food and lands on his feet, with mashed potatoes covering his thinning hair.

I interviewed Jonathan a few times on set. The final interview was on *Breaking Bad* episode 507, where Walter White shoots him and he dies by the river. It was a tough day for Jonathan because his character was being killed off after four years on the show. The crew wore black armbands all day to mourn for his characters demise. He didn't yet know that his character would be revived for five seasons on *Better Call Saul*.

Jonathan sat for a few interviews before this but he was choked up this day. It was to be his last. At first he said that he'd rather not do the interview, but he came around and asked if Bryan could sit with him to help him get through it. So they sat together, squabbling over a choice by his character like a married couple, as I tried to squeeze in an interview.

In the interview, Jonathan spoke from the heart. He was thankful for the great character and for the show. In the end he choked up, saying that this was "as good as it's ever been."

 See the interview on YouTube at : *Making of Breaking Bad Episode 507*

* * *

In interviews, the writing team on *Breaking Bad* and *Better Call Saul* often spoke of "listening" to their characters when crafting episodes. It's common knowledge that Aaron Paul was only planned for the first season but his connection with Bryan Cranston was tangible so they kept him on.

Lesser known is Jonathan Banks' long run as Mike. In the scene where Jesse's girlfriend, Jane, dies from an overdose the script called for Bob Odenkirk to save the day as a "cleaner." But Bob had a previous commitment and couldn't make the day. Enter Jonathan Banks, hired for just that day. But Jonathan was so magnetic that he stayed on until his demise midway through the fifth season and continued onto *Better Call Saul*.

* * *

In a later chapter, I speak of the Sky Warriors Project with military Veterans at CNM. My students and I had already shot all of the action shots of the Vets assembling, inflating, and flying the hot air balloon and we were plowing through the final interviews. But we didn't have an opening. I thought of Jonathan.

The next time I was on set I approached him. We were standing between takes when I made the pitch – "Hey, Jonathan. I'm working on a project with Vets…" Jonathan butted in, saying "Yes." I took a beat and chuckled. I hadn't begun to sell the job and he was all in. He listened as I explained the project. When I was done he said, "I already said yes."

We planned for Jonathan to stand with the Vets and make a statement to lead into the video. We shot on my front lawn with the CNM film students. I wrote a couple variations of an intro but he asked for some paper and sat at my desk. He wrote his own intro and joined us on the lawn.

Roll camera – Jonathan standing with 5 members of the Sky Warriors team and balloonist Diana Myklebust.

Cue Jonathan – "I'm Jonathan Banks. There are a group of people in this country I feel I owe a great debt to – our Veterans. Sometimes there's a peace above the earth, sometimes troubles are left behind. I would like to introduce you to the Sky Warriors."

Jonathan stayed awhile to chat with the vets like old friends.

 You can watch the video on my YouTube channel : https://www.youtube.com/@ chuckiedidit-sc3rm

* * *

As we broke down our equipment, a car pulled to the curb. My son, Keaton, was being dropped off by a US Marine recruiter. I introduced him to Jonathan. Hearing that he was joining the Marines, Jonathan invited him and the recruiter to spend a day as his guest on the set of *Breaking Bad*. Keaton was used to the industry, but this was all new to the recruiter, a Marine Staff Sergeant. They spent the day watching the crew shoot the show and were greeted by the show's stars as they sat with Jonathan at lunch. Jonathan's a kind and solid human being.

The Big Mistake – Happy Birthday !

We all make mistakes, some big some small, and the size of the mistake is directly connected to what you're working with. A mistake by a Nuclear Engineer will probably be more consequential than one made by a 7/11 clerk.

There were many producers on *Breaking Bad* and *Better Call Saul* and my hero was Stew Lyons. Stew was on top of everything and always hired the best in every department. So I felt honored when he asked me to run a weekend of show PR, still shots with the stars, and creating the show poster for *Better Call Saul*, featuring Bob standing at a pay phone in the desert with the receiver swinging in the wind. Look up the poster on-line. Bob is standing at the pay phone in a desert field, rich with tumbleweed, looking lonely and remote. In fact, Bob and the phone are only 15 yards from edge of the studio parking lot in Albuquerque.

Mid day we had a birthday celebration planned on the set for Michael McKean, Saul's older brother in the show. Michael is about as big as any star in the past thirty years. He was Lenny on *Laverne and Shirley*, and David St. Hubbins, lead guitarist in *This is Spinal Tap*. He's very respected.

On most sets we celebrate cast and crew birthdays with at least a sheet cake at craft services. On occasions, a star will gift a special treat for crew birthdays, like a gourmet coffee truck at midnight.

I ordered a sheet cake from a local bakery and sent a PA (production assistant) to pick it up. We had a table ready with a knife, plates and forks, and a space for the big cake. When the cake arrived the room was abuzz. Everyone but Michael were in on it. As the cake slid out of the box an AD started leading Michael towards the celebration. All that was left was to light the candles.

Oh shit, we don't have any candles. I can see Michael heading towards us and, just beyond the set, Bob Odenkirk has a handful of napkins and is trying with all his might to wrap them tight enough to stick into the cake so that he could light them. I was mortified !

As drastic as it seems, it was a small mistake on a large production, no big deal. So we ate the cake even though my hair had turned grey !

Breaking In On the Top Floor

Victoria Principal Is A Peach !

On my first big time TV experience in '87 I was hired on the pilot episode of *Sparks: The Price Of Passion* with Victoria Principal, Ted Wass, Grandpa Walton's Ralph Waite, *Pretty Woman's* Hector Elizondo and Broadway icon Elaine Stritch. Ms. Principal had purchased the screenplay and 13 'pay or play' episodes through her company, Victoria Principal Productions, serving as Executive Producer and leading lady, Albuquerque Mayor Patricia Sparks. Sadly the episodes did not get made.

I was 37, so I was old for a film set newbie, starting as the office PA. But the key PA got fired and I was moved to the set to replace him.

John Flynn, the 1st AD (Asst. Director), saw my drive and put me on the AD crew. And he added one instruction, there's a stalker threatening Victoria so you're to stay by her, just out of frame at all times. He went on to cheer me up about my new responsibility, saying "You wanna get ahead in the film biz, take a bullet for Victoria." WHAT !!! I knew that John was kidding but my wife was pissed.

My first day on the set was at a huge library hall at the University of New Mexico that was doubling as City Council Chambers. We were setting up for a medium close-up of Victoria as she exited the chamber's door. I was positioned to the right of the door, out of frame, ready to cue Victoria. The AD called "stand by" in my headset, so I called it out to the crew nearby. About ten feet away a makeup artist was doing 'final looks' on Victoria's makeup, slight tweaks just before the camera rolls. She wasn't done so Victoria caught my eye and said, "We need a minute."

I cued my radio and called to the AD, saying that Victoria needed a minute. Although we were already working together I hadn't been formally introduced to Ms. Principal. I nearly melted when she shot dagger eyes at me and declared … "Never say that you're waiting for me – don't ever fucking say that you're waiting for ME." HOLY SHIT ! It's my first day on set and I'm gonna be fired.

The makeup artist finished and we rolled the camera. My job was to cue Victoria's entrance. The AD called and I cued her. But as she passed me she reached out and punched me in the stomach, not really hard, she's tiny. But that was it. I was crestfallen. I'd made it to my first real professional gig and now I'd be fired.

John called "cut" and as we re-set for a second take, Victoria re-entered the chamber and wrapped her arms around me in a big hug. As she pulled away she said "I'm just playing with you 'cause you're more fun than that other guy." It was the first of many fun encounters with Victoria and a fabulous introduction to working with stars in the big time.

Usually stars are driven to and from the set by Teamsters but I was charged with driving her home some evenings. A couple times she invited me into her condo and we chatted like old friends, sipping homemade sweet tea in goblets. High Class !

* * *

One scene in the show was set at The Rock House, a primitive, single-room building made of stone with no roof, that sits on Sandia Peak overlooking Albuquerque. It's over 10,600 feet above sea level, and popular for teens drinking beer and smoking pot.

The scene was between Victoria and Ted Wass. Just as the AD called "cut" on the scene Victoria fainted from hypothermia. Luckily, I was just a step out of frame and caught her as she fell. I know that my mom told that tale to friends until she was blue in the face.

* * *

In production we sometimes shoot long tracking shots – someone walking, driving or riding a horse. The shot can be used to cover a transition or to stretch time. In the film

Superfly director Gordon Parks used driving shots to fill time since the script was short for a feature production.

We took Victoria and a classic old pickup truck with a split windshield to the desert on the West side of town – tumbleweeds rolling to forever. I was positioned with Victoria about a hundred yards from the camera, ready to cue her. She was to drive on this lonely dirt trail as the camera panned, revealing the vast, open space. The camera rolled, Victoria started to drive and I ran like a bat outta hell to get out of the frame. But there was nowhere to hide, the panning camera revealed the emptiness. That's when the AD yelled "Dive, Charlie." I dove onto a small cactus – ouch. A small sacrifice to get the shot.

As we packed up our equipment to leave we were visited by three Sheriff's deputies who drove up in a panicked cloud of dust. Apparently a nosy local saw our commotion and reported that we were burying bodies. The Sheriffs didn't buy our story, that we were shooting a film, until one of the deputies recognized Victoria, standing with me to the side. With apologies all around, we laughed together and went on with our day.

* * *

Sparks was a pilot for a TV series. The art department stored props and wardrobe in a garage for their return, but the series wasn't picked up, meaning the production was over. I got a call from the producer asking me to ship the items back to them in LA. I had helped move the items into storage and knew that they were leftovers and didn't see any wisdom incurring the shipping costs. There was nothing they could use. I suggested that I could sell the items locally and send them a check. They agreed and asked me to do just that.

Most of the items were small, hand props and clothing. There was an old covered wagon, a real one, that I sold to a restaurant, a wild west icon for their front lawn. I deposited the cash and sent a check to LA.

A week or so later the check came back to me in the mail, uncashed, with VOID and "Merry Christmas" scrawled across it. The check was for over $1,500. For a young dad, it was Merry Christmas indeed.

The Raffle – *Young Guns II*

A great side benefit in the film biz is getting to work with giants of the industry. One of the many producers on *Young Guns II* was Irby Smith. Irby was the First AD on *One Flew Over The Cuckoo's Nest* and *Stand By Me.* I worked with him again on *City Slickers.*

We were shooting in a false front western town near Santa Fe and he had an issue to solve. He had welcomed families of crew members to watch production but many were following the crew to lunch. On location in 1990 meals were served in a huge tent by amazing caterers, and it was expensive, like $20 bucks a plate plus expenses, and worth it. But there was no budget for set visitor lunches.

Irby had an idea. He asked me to get a roll of tickets and pass them out to crew members so they would have to present a 'ticket' to get lunch. CRAP ! It was a good idea but I knew that the crew would laugh at me. I envisioned a burly grip tossing the ticket in the dirt while declaring a version of "we don't need no stinkin' badges" to my face. So I improvised.

I got a set of raffle tickets, a double roll with matching numbers. One ticket goes to the holder and one goes into a hat for the raffle. The idea was to fulfill Irby's request in a way the crew would accept. But now I had a raffle to run. I needed prizes.

I had a naked Barbie in my trunk that I'd rescued from my sons, a good start. I turned to the varied departments looking for prizes. Special Effects donated a dozen condoms they use for squirting blood hits. The game was on. I told the crew to keep their tickets for the lunchtime raffle.

Once the crew were seated with their meals I announced the raffle to a skeptical crew. They rolled their eyes and groaned. What the hell is this ? But then I started. The first prize that I offered was the naked Barbie and it went to one of our stars, Emilio Estevez. The mood changed instantly as Emilio accepted the doll as if it was an Oscar with a short speech. Somebody won the condoms and an electrician won an oversized pair of Disney boxer shorts from wardrobe. The game was on, indeed.

It was such a hit that Irby charged me with running the raffle daily at lunch, with joke prizes and a petty cash line for prize purchases. The crew responded, bringing donations to add to the fun. The DP donated an expensive bottle of champagne after he won some silly prize. Emilio gifted the Barbie to the camera department and she sat spread-eagled on the 'A' camera lens for a day or two.

Years later I resurrected the raffle on *The Fight Before Christmas,* a joint German/Italian comedy produced for the European market. The Germans and Italians were constantly at odds, so the raffle was a welcome break.

Ruth Buzzi* of *Laugh-In* fame was in the show and gladly joined in, picking the winning tickets out of a prop hat. She was a joy !

* * *

My first encounter with the *Young Guns II* cast was in the production office. I was an office PA, prepping for principal photography to start.

Our offices were a string of hotel rooms with connecting doors that maintenance removed for our convenience. My desk was next to the door to the producer's office. There was a steady hum of activity.

Suddenly, a tornado of testosterone swept into the room, bypassed my desk, and swirled into the producer's office. It was the excitable young cast, Emilio Estevez, Kiefer Sutherland, Lou Diamond Phillips and Christian Slater. They must have flown into Santa Fe on the same plane.

I was too intimidated to look in as the air filled with crashing sounds, lasting about five minutes. The tornado swept out of the offices with equal fury. What the hell ?

I had to see what they'd done. In five minutes the guys had turned EVERYTHING upside down – the desks, TV, bookshelves and filing cabinets were all upended, a real mess. Can you imagine the clutter left behind when filing cabinets are set on their heads. So much for efficient records. But it was all in fun, young stars pranking their bosses. No worries.

* * *

The film was produced by Morgan Creek Productions, owned by James G. Robinson. One day Jim called with a concern. There was a minor in the cast, Balthazar Getty, grandson of multi-gazillionaire J. Paul Getty, owner of Getty Oil. Balthazar was fifteen so he couldn't party in bars with the rest of the cast. Jim asked me to secure an extra hotel room and have a pool table delivered so that Balthazar could play whenever he pleased.

I decided to go a step further. Most of the cast and visiting crew were housed in the hotel, but the big wigs had condos next door. I rented a condo on the company dime, had the pool table delivered, and called other cast members to see what 'toys' they'd like in their game room. I remember that Emilio wanted a race car arcade game and I got it for him.

The game room was for cast only, so I had keys made for each of them and, while I was at it, made a key for myself. I was a PA but I was in my late thirties and full of piss and vinegar, so why not. One evening at wrap I went to the condo. Emilio was on the race car game and Kiefer was shooting pool by himself. I asked if I could join him and he welcomed me. A pretty woman was sitting to the side.

After a short time Kiefer introduced me to his date, Julia. I greeted her and played on. It wasn't until later that I realized that it was Julia Roberts.

Julia wasn't a household name yet BUT she'd just been nominated for a Best Supporting Actress Oscar for her role in *Steel Magnolias.* The next day I approached her on set and congratulated her for her nomination. She was very gracious, a Pretty Woman, indeed.

The people you run into !

* * *

Back to the film: Christian Slater has a gunfight with a lawman, both on horseback. He rides his horse into a china shop, firing through the windows at the lawman in the street. As he spins his horse to duck shots we see the china exploding off of the shelves all around him.

After the scene was wrapped there were about thirty plates and bowls left, undamaged. The decoration on the plates was designed to mimic the Old West time period. I bought the leftover dishes, planning to prank my mom.

My son, Keaton, had just been born so my parents had flown from Philly to meet him. Johanna, Miles, Keaton and me were living in her brother's New Mexico style house with Saltillo tile floors in the kitchen and stucco walls, sturdy. Johanna and I were actors in our past and we devised a plan. I stacked the dishes in a box with a damaged bowl on top. These were special effects dishes, never fired in a kiln, so they broke easily. My dad had heart issues so we clued him in on the gag.

I told mom that we'd purchased some new, special dishes, and wanted her to see them. I carried the box to the kitchen and set it on the counter.

Immediately I grabbed the chipped bowl and confronted Johanna: "This bowl is chipped, can't we have anything nice" ? I smashed the bowl on the floor. Johanna yelled, picked up a plate and threw it at me. We continued until the floor was covered in broken plates. My mom couldn't take it and left the room. I found her in the guest bedroom by the window, praying for us.

I tried to tell her that it was a gag but she couldn't listen. I gently took her by the hand and brought her back to the kitchen where I explained that these were stunt dishes and it was all a joke. To convince her, I grabbed one of the remaining plates and broke it over my head. She laughed so hard that tears were streaming down her cheeks.

That's the kind of family we are.

Can ya straighten out that hill ?

Back in the day, before films were chock full of special effects, there were simple tricks of the trade to make things seem different than they were. One 'trick' is a dutch angle. Tilting the camera to exaggerate the frame.

On *Young Guns II,* Lou Diamond Philips and Kiefer Sutherland are escaping on horseback. The script called for them to ride headlong down a steep hill, risking their horses and their own lives. To make the scene safe for the actors a few tricks were employed. Locations made an agreement with the San Felipe Pueblo, south of Santa Fe, to shoot on a hill with a modest slope, dotted with piñon bushes. With the approval of the tribe, the greens crew* shaved off one side of each bush and the DP (director of photography) tilted the camera for a Dutch angle thus exaggerating the steepness of the hill.

On "action" Lou and Kiefer laid back as if straining to make the grade and rode down the hill. It was very safe but looked dangerous. I'm certain that production paid a pretty penny to the tribe. A similar scene had been shot years before for *The Man From Snowy River* but their production chose to let the actors drive their horses down a truly steep incline, killing one of the horses.

We also shot at Tent Rocks, a desert location with tall rock and sand formations jutting upward from the ground, looking like a series of Teepees. Kasha-Katuwe, Tent Rocks National Monument, is a precious and protected site South of Santa Fe. After filming, production was charged $15,000 in re-seeding fees. Our trucks had done more damage than anticipated.

Most film productions are good stewards of the land, realizing that they're on somebody's property, like guests in their home, and guarantee to leave every site in as good or better condition than when they arrive.

Lou Diamond Phillips

This is a special relationship spanning twenty-plus years. Let me explain.

The first time I worked with Lou he was one of the stars in *Young Guns II*. He had a scene early in the script where he and Kiefer Sutherland were taken from jail to be hanged by a gang of vigilantes. They were being escorted out of town by an angry mob wearing white sheets and hoods. As they rode, the gang leader taunted them through his hooded mask.

But the switch was afoot as he pulled off his hood – it was Billy The Kid, Emilio Estevez, and they were saved. But in true Western style, the tables turn as the real vigilantes ride into town. A gunfight ensues.

Lou and Emilio ducked into an alley between old wooden buildings. The scene was written for Billy the Kid to shoot the handcuffs off of Lou's wrists and escape together.

But mistakes were made. Lou was on horseback with a set of handcuffs restricting his arms and a noose around his neck that was tied around the saddle horn. Who dreamed up this scenario ?

The planned action was simple: Lou would lift his arms, Emilio would shoot off the handcuffs, and they'd escape. Not so fast.

It sounds simple but to create realism the special effects (FX) crew have a lot to do. Since Emilio is firing a blank, you need an FX shooter to fire a dust pellet into the wall to simulate the bullet strike. The handcuffs have a tiny explosive set off by another FX expert making it look like a bullet broke the chain.

But the commotion led the horse to spook and run off with Lou.

Realizing that the rope around his neck was tied to the saddle horn, Lou freed the rope and leapt off the horse. But the toe of his boot got stuck in the stirrup and the horse dragged him across 30 yards of desert, repeatedly slamming his head and body on the hard ground.

Again, mistakes were made. It would have been wise to complete the sequence with a wrangler just out of frame holding the horse's bridle, but that was overlooked. So, when the horse spooked, there was no one to stop him.

Lucky for Lou there was a lone wrangler just 30 yards away and the horse ran straight to him and stopped.

The set medic rushed to Lou, lying unconscious. I rushed to help. We cut off his clothes searching for injuries. At first the medic noticed blood on the back of Lou's head from being dragged, but we ultimately determined that Lou's elbow had been crushed when the horse smashed him against a fencepost.

The producers called in a helicopter to fly Lou to The University of New Mexico Medical Center, a trauma 1 hospital. An enterprising woman in town bought a set of nurse's scrubs and snuck into his room for an autograph. The script had to be revised since the opening scene with Lou hadn't been shot yet.

That was in 1990. Jump forward 22 years and Lou is in Las Vegas, New Mexico, to shoot the pilot for *Longmire*, a modern western set in Montana but shot in New Mexico. Lou was cast as the Native American owner of the local watering hole, The Red Pony, and close friend to the Sheriff, Walt Longmire.

I'd been hired to shoot behind the scenes and film interviews with the stars, the producers and the director. I'd scored rooms for my crew at the classic Plaza Hotel, ready to shoot the next day.

As I entered the hotel lobby, I saw Lou across the room. It was too good an opportunity to pass up. I approached him with outstretched hand and greeted him with "Howdy, Lou – the last time I saw you was 20 years ago when I was cutting off your clothes."

Lou released my hand and took a small step backwards, separating himself from me with a cautious smile. I cracked up. When I explained, Lou breathed a sigh of relief and bought me a beer.

Side note – Lou was unconscious as we cut off his clothes, looking for wounds. But three times he came back to life, lifted his head and asked "Did we get the shot?" only to drop back into his unconscious state.

Jon Bon Jovi

A pivotal scene in the beginning of *Young Guns II* has Kiefer Sutherland and Lou escaping from a rustic jail cell, a hole in the ground with eight other grungy men, huddled against the cold. One cowboy meets the business end of a double-barreled shotgun as he tries to escape. That's Jon Bon Jovi.

The *Young Guns II* cast was a showcase for young, hot talent – Kiefer and Lou, Christian Slater, Emilio Estevez, William Peterson, Viggo Mortensen and Balthazar Getty.

Bon Jovi sang the movie's theme, *Blaze of Glory*, and showed up in Santa Fe to hang out with the cast. The guys insisted he appear in the film and talked him into costume.

The director set up a scene where Jon would be shot while escaping the muddy cell and fall back into the hole, a quick cameo, easy. We shot the first angle then broke for lunch. Scenes are shot from varied angles to create a flow in the edit.

On our return from lunch the AD crew couldn't find the extra, the background actor, who was escaping next to Bon Jovi. They needed him to match the shot. Without hesitation the 1st AD called for me to get suited up to replace him and do a scene with Bon Jovi.

Tough Day !? Forced to play a scene with a rock star ! Sadly, only my ass is recognizable in the frame.

Film Industry Jobs

Here's a primer on industry jobs before you scroll to the Appendix.

I was first a PA, production assistant, or pack animal if the producer is a slave driver. The PA is at the bottom of the totem pole. They're a gopher at the start but, with experience, a PA can be tasked with setting "places" for background extras and cueing their movements. The key PA is the head of the gophers.

Production Coordinator – the coordinator runs the office. They're in contact with vendors to order supplies and equipment, and are responsible for disseminating call sheets to the cast and crew, and completing a production report at the end of each day.

AD – Assistant Director – the AD runs the set in support of the director. It's a management job, not creative. On commercials there's often just one AD but on feature films and TV series there's a first AD, second AD, and second second AD, with detailed responsibilities spelled out in union rules.

I was also a producer/director with my own company, Working Boy Productions, producing local and regional commercials, including all the Public Safety videos for the state of New Mexico.

EPK Producer – I'll often speak of interviewing cast members, directors and department heads. EPK stands for Electronic Press Kit. During filming an EPK crew is sent to shoot background footage and conduct interviews to be used for marketing the project. Clips are offered to shows like *Good Morning America* and the like to promote the film. Think about it, by the time a film is released the actors have gone on to other projects. The EPK footage shows the actors during production months earlier, and is deployed when the film is released.

On the fifth season of *Breaking Bad*, AMC and Sony upped the ante, tasking my crew with creating a five minute 'making of' video for each episode. Each of my videos was shown on AMC following that week's episode.

You can see all 16 videos on YouTube at : *Making of Breaking Bad Episode 501* (through episode 516)

Dancing With The Doorknob

I was a young pup growing up in a Philly suburb. A TV show was airing across the country covering the latest in pop music and dance crazes – *American Bandstand* – shot live in Philly.

Because the show was taped in our hometown we took to it daily like mother's milk. Every day after school we'd rush in the house, sling our backpacks on the couch and crank the TV. Every teen that I knew danced away the afternoon to the national dance party hosted by Dick Clark.

I was in my early teens and a bit awkward so my older sister refused to dance with me, that's where the doorknob comes in. Variations on the jitterbug were still very popular so you actually touched your partner. It's not easy to do the jitterbug alone, but so much of the dance relies on holding your partner's hand as you launch each other to and fro. So, wanting to dance but with no partner, I recruited the doorknob of the dining room closet. Grabbing the knob I'd spin out, always returning to a firm grip on the nob. A little less than romantic, but a useful substitute for a gawky 13-year-old.

Some years later Dick Clark moved his production to LA, a loss for Philly. But an enterprising local DJ named Hy Lit filled the gap with a similar dance show broadcast to the local market plus parts of New Jersey, New York and Delaware, *The Hy Lit Show*. By that time I was in high school and decidedly more cool. A bunch of us teens from the suburbs chartered a bus to take us to the studio in town. Yikes, we were dancing on TV !

The Hy Lit Show was broadcast from '67 to '70. Clips from the show are online on YouTube.

Pop stars from Chubby Checkers to The Delfonics were featured on the show, lip-syncing to their hits. Check out all of the young Catholic school students swooning to Marvin Gaye and Tammi Terrell as they lip-synced *Ain't No Mountain High Enough.*

I had two younger sisters, Terri and Annie, 11 and 13 years younger than me respectively. They were around five and seven at the time and they were baffled. How was it possible to watch their brother on TV while sitting next to him on the couch ?

Saturated in the dance craze, the student council at my high school, Monsignor Bonner in Upper Darby, started a Saturday night mixer. Hundreds of juniors and seniors from the surrounding schools rocked out.

I won at least 30 dance contests over the course of a couple of years and cherished the prizes, compilation albums gathered by local DJs with 22 varied hits.

I'm sad to say that my mom donated the albums with my comic books and baseball cards to a church yard sale. What those baseball cards would be worth today ! And where else will I find a recording of *I'm a Lonely Frog* by Clarence 'Frogman' Henry ?

I still love you, Mom !

Raising Sons On Set

I have two sons – glorious, smart, handsome sons, Miles and Keaton. Any child gets to experience some of whatever their parents do in their day job, creating memories. But some "jobs" are more interesting than others. On that scale, filmmaking is pretty exciting.

I did a lot of work for New Mexico State Government. There were public safety commercials of all kinds, DWI, forest fire safety, Click It or Ticket (seat belts), accessible parking (handicapped), and more.

In 2008 I was asked to shoot a message about health care featuring the Lieutenant Governor, Dianne Denish. It was up to me to create a background for the spot, otherwise you have a talking head and no visual interest for the viewer. They leave the room and make a sandwich.

I always created small stories, 30-second stories to wrap the message in. I learned that approach from Dave and Barry at Southwest Productions. More on them later. My head was spinning with ideas for the shoot. A fun part about filmmaking is locations, being welcomed into homes and businesses to create an atmosphere for your story.

South of town investors had built the Albuquerque Studios. Eight state-of-the-art film sound stages, half with 50-foot ceilings. They were as good as any stage in LA. But, for us locals, they were off limits unless you were working on a show or invited to a set.

A new show, *Breaking Bad*, was filming its first season at the studios. I wanted to be there or, as Liz Lemon would say "I want to go to there."

So I hatched a plan.

I called the producer of *Breaking Bad*, Stew Lyons, and floated the idea that he could gain some points with the Lieutenant Governor if we could shoot her message on a set. *Breaking Bad* was shooting in Albuquerque in large part due to the state's tax incentives. Sucking up a little would be smart.

Then I called the Lt. Governor and floated the idea that she could get the VIP treatment at the new film studios if we shot there. I was thrilled when both Stew and Diane bought the plan.

Side note: In film classes I always spoke of the use of manipulation, justifications and old-fashioned sucking up to move production forward. You're dealing with countless unique, creative people, and the clock is ticking. How do you get from here to there without abusing anyone's ego? There's often space for a juicy manipulation. It's OK when you have a kind heart and no one's rushed to the ER.

Prepping for the shoot, I wrote a 30-second script. I staged a scene like a classic TV detective show, casting a Broderick Crawford detective type, holding a gun on a suspect. After about 5 seconds a director calls "cut" and the actors relax as the Lt. Governor steps into frame with her message. We shot the scene in the backyard patio of

Walter White's house on the *Breaking Bad* set. Stew came to the set and greeted Lt. Gov. Denish.

My son, Keaton, was on set helping with craft services, on set snacks. At some point I noticed Bryan Cranston looking in on us. We all knew him as the dad from *Malcolm in the Middle*, no one knew who Walter White was yet.

At home that night, Keaton told me that, while I was busy with the shoot, he sat and chatted with Bryan for about twenty minutes. Picture that, a 16-year-old kid face to face with a star from his favorite show. He had the best story at school the next day.

* * *

A few times my boys got cast in jobs because the casting director knew them through me.

In 1998 Reynolds Tobacco company got spanked in court. They were ordered to pay a boatload of money to fund education initiatives to stop kids from smoking, a billion dollars, no shit. Part of the settlement paid to film ads for TV and the internet. Local casting director, Kathy Brink, called to offer Miles a shoot day on one of the commercials. It paid 150 bucks. Miles was 14.

On occasion I hired the boys to work as PAs on my shoots and paid them well, like a hundred bucks for being a gopher. So I figured that Miles would jump at the chance. I told him that he'd be paid a hundred fifty bucks, expecting him to light up. But he declined. I followed that he'd get the day off from school and that worked.

Miles was always a clown, a loud clown, like me. On the shoot day I hung around the set to watch production. The director was pairing different teens in shots with short dialogue, varying the looks. At one point I heard Miles rambling on about me, "My dad's a director," and it was annoying.

So the AD removed Miles from the shot. Miles never realized that he'd been dismissed for his disruptive behavior. A true clown, he was safe in his own world, not noticing that he'd been, in fact, fired. But he still got paid so the day ended in the plus column. A hundred and fifty bucks.

A month or so later we received a SAG contract, Screen Actors Guild. The commercial was a union shoot so Miles was offered the chance to join. We declined, knowing that he'd have to join the next time he got a speaking role. No big deal.

Then the checks started rolling in.

Residual payment is based on media buys. Every time they booked the ad for a 13-week run on a network, Miles got paid. The same rules applied to ad buys on the internet. We had no idea that this would be part of the deal.

The checks averaged a thousand bucks each time. In the following 18 months, Miles pocketed $35,000, a windfall for a teenager. The only drawback was that we never saw the ad.

So I contacted the agency, told them the story, and asked for a copy of the ad. They were very accommodating.

A week or so later a VHS copy arrived in the mail. Miles sat with great anticipation as I popped the tape into the VCR. The video started with color bars, then the black and white 3, 2, 1 countdown, then on came the teens but... Miles wasn't in it ! WHAT ? He got paid $35,000 and he wasn't even in the spot !

Love them union rules !

Billy Crystal and Ted Bundy

Billy Crystal & *City Slickers*

I worked with Billy on *City Slickers* in 1991, also starring Bruno Kirby, Daniel Stern, Jack Palance, Helen Slater, Josh Mostel, David Paymer, Noble Willingham and Jake Gyllenhall.

Billy is a gentleman, an enormously talented actor and a precious human. Check out his comic routine on YouTube from 1979 where he channels Mohamad Ali and Howard Cossell at a tribute to Ali. He repeated some of the skit during his tribute at Ali's funeral to the delight of Ali's family.

We shot part of *City Slickers* in Durango, Colorado and the rest in Santa Fe and Abiqui, New Mexico, famous for Georgia O'Keefe and her paintings of the mountains and desert.

Billy was a producer on the film as well as the lead actor. I was young in my film career and yearned for personal time with him. It was my job to run the production office and to set up offices for the producers and the director. So I arranged for an office that Billy would share with producer Irby Smith*. In the layout, Billy would have to pass my desk to get to his office. In those two months in Durango he never came to his office. He was too busy on set. Damn! So much for my plan.

In Durango we shot the end of the cattle drive including the river crossing where Billy saves Norman, the calf, from being swept away. The Army Corps of Engineers assisted production, lowering the water level by controlling the flow from an upstream dam to mitigate the danger for the cast and crew.

I finally got some face time with Billy once we moved production to the Garson Studios* in Santa Fe. The Garson Studios was perfect. There were production offices for the company plus two stages, so the stars and shooting crew were all there, unless they were on location.

At the Garson, I positioned my desk at the front door. Everybody had to deal with me, and that led to fun moments with Billy, Jack Palance, Danny Stern, Bruno Kirby, David Paymer and Josh Mostel.

One day Billy was waiting to be called to the set. He sat by my desk and we chatted. His daughter, Lindsay, was in the show and she was excited about the horses. Some of her friends had horses and Billy swore up and down that he wouldn't go down that road. Of course he loved the kid and would do anything for her, but he knew many friends who shlepped the two-hour round trip from their home in

Belair to the horse stable somewhere in Canyon Country. Not for him.

Billy was called to set just as my phone rang, honest to God ! It was one of Billy's managers. She had just bought his horse from the show and asked if I'd get producer Irby Smith to present it to him.

Studio B at the Garson had been transformed into a rock canyon, with 20-foot walls made of a wood frame, chicken wire, plaster and paint. And it was a full circle. One section swung out on wheels to get the crew in.

I'm no dummy, so I joined Irby to present the horse to Billy. I don't remember how we got Billy to join us in the canyon, but the three of us turned as a wrangler entered the canyon set with Billy's horse.

It would be a gross understatement to say that Billy was moved. A set photographer started to shoot the scene and Irby put a stop to it. This was personal.

Billy was choked up as he stroked his gorgeous horse. You may remember a similar scene from *M.A.S.H.* where Radar O'Reilly presents a horse to Colonel Potter. Potter cried, too.

The next year Billy rode the horse onto the stage as the opening to his Oscar monologue, with the orchestra playing the *City Slickers* theme.

* * *

Why go to the expense of building a canyon indoors ? Why not just shoot in a canyon ? Well, it was a night scene, in November in Santa Fe, very cold. Building the canyon on a stage meant that we were shooting indoors in the daytime and faking the darkness. No weather worries. No sick actors or crew.

* * *

On another occasion Billy sat by my desk to chat. A PA entered the front door of the studios pushing a hand cart heavy with cases of copy paper. Billy expressed concern that the film industry wasted so much paper. I agreed and told him that, in response, I planted a tree for every film that I worked on. He smiled.

A few days later Billy brought me a young tree. It was a Ponderosa pine. I planted it at the head of the driveway on my brother-in-law's property in the mountains of Cedar Crest, New Mexico. Thirty years later the tree is about 25 feet tall and robust.

* * *

For the opening scenes of *City Slickers* construction built a working ranch in an open field on the Ghost Ranch property in Abiquiu. They built a ranch house, a barn, corrals, an open horse arena, and a small store where Billy, Bruno and Danny try on appropriate cowboy fashion, a comic montage in the film.

Film productions pay location fees wherever they shoot, but an added benefit is the improvements made to the property, such as new buildings. Often buildings play as exteriors only and the property owner can flesh out the interior after production wraps. That was the case with *City Slickers* on Ghost Ranch. The barn was built for exteriors only but the store and ranch house had completed interiors. The location contract specified that the buildings would be gifted to the ranch with the stipulation that they wouldn't be used for any future production, a huge gift. But shortly after the film wrapped, Ghost Ranch allowed a Toyota commercial to be filmed on the set. Castle Rock sued, forcing Ghost Ranch to demolish the buildings at their expense.

* * *

Although the ranch house was built with interior shots in mind, those scenes were scrapped and the set dressing was sold. I was fortunate to buy an oak dining room set, a table with leaves and six chairs, for a quarter of their retail value, and surprised my wife with the set for Thanksgiving. The classic oak set replaced the six-foot folding table we'd been using. Much classier.

* * *

In the film, Billy and Jack Palance peel off from the group to find cattle that had strayed. They bunk together overnight in the woods where Billy plays his harmonica by the fire, annoying Jack. The scene was shot indoors on

Stage A at the Garson Studios. Set dressing supplied 25 mature pine trees, numerous big rocks made of styrofoam and tons of dirt, literally tons. Again, better to build a set and shoot indoors than to risk the actors' health for a cold, night shoot.

Back on location in the morning, they find a pregnant cow struggling to give birth. Jack springs into action, telling Billy that they have to assist with the birth, leaving Billy to reach up inside the cow and pull out her calf while Jack subdues the mother. The scene was a seamless marriage of special effects and real life. The calf that Billy pulls out is real while the rear half of the mother cow was a styrofoam replica. A crew member pushed the calf out towards Billy with an oversized toilet plunger.

The FX crew went on to create dozens of styrofoam bison lying dead on the plains in *Dances With Wolves*. I worked with a member of the same team decades later creating FX makeup on Aaron Paul's badly beaten face in the final season of *Breaking Bad*.

* * *

I've already mentioned that set dressing and other assets are often sold after wrap. The task was somewhat larger on *City Slickers*. What do you do with a herd of cattle you no longer need ? Sell them to a local burger chain, of course.

Our herd was sold to a family-owned burger chain, What-A-Burger. I'll take two with ketchup and pickles.

My film students freaked out when I told them – they groaned "those poor cows." What else are you going to do with them ? Take 50 head of cattle home as pets !?

The calf that Billy births and then rescues was named "Norman". There were 12 calves purchased to play Norman at different ages and sizes.

* * *

Billy has two kids in the story, a boy and a girl. The girl was played by Billy's daughter, Lindsay, and the boy was played by Jake Gyllenhaal, his first film at five years old. Jake's scenes were shot in LA and NY so I didn't get to meet him. Decades later I worked with his dad, director Stephen Gyllenhaal, shooting background plates for a feature film that was never funded. The DP on the project was Michael Chapman, famed for shooting *Raging Bull, Taxi Driver* and *The Fugitive.* I'd work with Michael years later on *Suspect Zero*.

The Unknown Soldier

In 1980 I was a theater student at UNM when I happened upon a play by Peter Ustinov, *The Unknown Soldier and His Wife.* It's an anti-war comedy with five iconic characters that guarantee continual wars : there's the unknown soldier, his pregnant wife, the sergeant who runs the war, the general who starts the wars, and the archbishop who blesses the troops as they march off to war and sleeps with the general's wife while he's gone.

The country was heavy with anti-war sentiment at the time, so I convinced my mentor, Daddy Bob Hurtung, to stage the play. I was thrilled that he agreed and hoped to be cast as the archbishop, the role that Ustinov had written for himself. Bob had two actors vying for the role: Tim Nelson, a brilliant comedian, and myself. The auditions were grueling. I say auditions in plural because Bob put Tim and I head-to-head five times. It was a teaching moment but quite stressful. In the end, I was cast.

To ease the lasting tension I treated myself to a tune-up at my chiropractors. Ahhhhhhh – so relaxing. I was a poor college student without a car so I rode a bike for transportation. Leaving the doctor's office I felt refreshed, once again filled with piss and vinegar. So confident that I was riding with no hands on the handlebars. Of course I crashed, slamming my shoulder into the pavement.

I headed straight back to the doctor. He treated me again and stated that I had a sprained collarbone. He put my arm in a sling and told me to keep it there for the coming weeks.

The next day I saw Bob and told him of my accident, standing there with my arm in the sling. Bob took no prisoners. He told me in no uncertain terms that the archbishop had to raise his arms over his head in gestures to God throughout the play and that I couldn't do it with the sling. He gave me a choice: keep the sling and lose the part or lose the sling. I lost the sling. I still have a lump on my shoulder from the accident, another war wound.

Bob was a great and supportive director. He was the only director I knew who demanded that actors memorize their parts before the first rehearsal. In the theater that's called being 'off book.' It's hard to direct actors who stroll around the stage in rehearsal with their script in hand. We had to be off book from the start. I had to study.

I knew there were too many distractions at home, so I hopped a plane to my parents' house in Philly. But, realizing that I couldn't focus there, either, I hopped a train to the inner city and found a park near City Hall. I studied my part for a couple hours until I was cross-eyed. To clear my head, I walked around the park.

Philly is old school, bathed in history. Every park, street and building is named for or dedicated to somebody from the past. I looked for a plaque describing the park's origin. Low and behold the entire park was a graveyard for Unknown Soldiers from the Civil War. What were the chances ???

* * *

The play was a success and was nominated regionally for the American College Theater Festival, a national competition for college theater programs. The set was enormous, a replica of the Tomb of the Unknown Soldier in Arlington National Cemetery. We had to dismantle it, truck it sixty miles to the College of Santa Fe, and rebuild it on their stage for the competition.

The judges were three theater reviewers from respected newspapers. We were late getting the stage ready, finally starting over an hour late. At the end of the play the cast gets out of costume and meets with the reviewers. But we'd been late, so we went straight to the review in costume and makeup. The reviewers had poker faces, hard to read. Finally the reviewer from the St. Louis Post Dispatch spoke for the team. He was pissed.

He railed that we'd held up the process, making them cool their heels for an hour, setting the whole day's schedule back. Then he got to the point.

He said that their purpose was to give critical advice to both students and the director in case the play was moving on to the National Competition at the Kennedy Center, and there was nothing, nothing they could say to make our play better. Holy shit ! At that point the reviewers smiled and congratulated us. We had won the day. Daddy Bob was a great director. We were moving on in the competition to the Kennedy Center in D.C.

Unfortunately, UNM was in a bind. Money was tight and the school also wanted to send the football team to play the University of Hawaii in Oahu. You guessed it, the football team traveled, and lost, and we stayed home and licked our wounds.

On the bright side we were nominated as an ensemble cast for the Irene Ryan Award, the highest honor in college acting. Irene Ryan was an accomplished actress best known for playing Granny on *The Beverly Hillbillies* at the end of a glorious career.

But our loss wasn't just the trip to DC. Here we were in the desert of New Mexico, relatively unknown in the theater world with a world-class director. When you play at the Kennedy Center there are Broadway scouts in the house. A huge opportunity to be "discovered." I guess it just wasn't to be.

In Search Of : Possession

The TV show *In Search Of:* came to New Mexico to shoot a segment about a five-year-old boy who was possessed by some evil force and the exorcist who saved him. The parents of the boy had written a book on the experience and were in Santa Fe to receive a book award. The book is entitled *Enlightened Through Darkness* and is available on Amazon.

The production company enlisted a good friend, Rebecca Elise, to find the cast; a boy, a dad, and a woman to play the exorcist. She saw numerous boys but found the subject was beyond the capabilities of a five-year-old actor. So she called me and asked to audition Keaton for the part. Keaton was nine but skinny, looking younger than his age.

The producer of the show was doubling as director and loved Keaton. She enumerated the challenge : for Keaton to mimic anger and distress resulting from the possession. She hoped that he could lie on the floor and arch his back as if an entity was lifting him up by his belly. I approached the producer, telling her that I was a director and, with her permission, would coach him in preparing for the part. She accepted my offer and then added: "Just show him *The Exorcist* to see how Linda Blair did it." WHAT ? Show an impressionable nine-year-old *The Exorcist* ! No Way !

But Keaton took the role seriously and worked with me to prepare. Like any feisty nine-year-old, it wasn't a stretch for him to act out of control. Keaton got paid, but the kicker was that the producer cast me as the dad, so Keaton got to abuse me while the camera was rolling and got paid for it. Rough day, getting paid to pound on your father. In his pretend rage he stood on the back of the couch, leapt on my back, and started pounding on my head and neck.

The real exorcist was there as a consultant. I was intrigued. The real dad told us of their struggle with their son, seeking help that fell short until they found the exorcist. On the day they met her, she asked for an accounting of their experience. The dad spoke of a stuffed bear that somehow affected their son. The exorcist took charge, telling the dad that he needed to get the stuffed bear out of the house.

She instructed him to put the bear in their trash can and then watch as the garbage men emptied the can into their truck. Then watch as the blade scooped the bear up into the belly of the truck. The dad watched as the bear disappeared, relieved that this part of the nightmare was over. A few days later the father found the bear back on the boy's bed. Scary !

Side note: The casting agent on the production was Rebecca Elise. We had worked together for years at Southwest Productions so she knew Keaton well. Last night I told Keaton that I included this episode in the book. He revealed that when Rebecca offered him the role he accepted with one condition, that I would play his father. The shoot was scheduled for Father's Day and he wanted to spend the day with me. He's a keeper !

Randy Savage – The Macho Man

Southwest Productions produced tons of national commercials – Aleve, Slim Jims, multiple Proctor and Gamble products and dozens more.

The Slim Jims spots featuring 'The Macho Man Randy Savage' were lots of fun to shoot. For anyone from another planet, Randy was a star on the pro wrestling circuit. You might remember his tagline, "Snap into a Slim Jim !" He delivered the line in his animated, gruff voice. Selma Diamond* has nuthin' on Randy !

The last time we worked with Randy the commercial called for a fake wrestling scenario with Randy body slamming a skinny kid. We contracted for a pro wrestling ring to be set up in the Albuquerque Convention Center. As AD for the shoots, I always had personal moments with the talent. Randy and I were set friends. This was the fifth year working with him.

In a lull between shots Randy asked me how my kids were doing. I told him that they were struggling in school due to the craziness of the divorce they were living through. Randy got a brain fart. He asked if I had a personal video camera and told me to bring it to the shoot the next day. OK ?

I showed up with my camera the next day and approached Randy. He told me to hand the camera to Barry, the DP, and then step aside. I still had no idea what he was planning.

I know that at some point everyone has seen a clip of wrestlers trash-talking about their next match in a TV promo, very loud and threatening and straight at the camera. Randy and Barry climbed into the ring. Barry rolled the camera and Randy went on a rant, loudly challenging Miles and Keaton to knuckle down and do good in school in the same tone he'd use to intimidate an opponent.

He ranted that he and I were tag team partners for life and he'd be on the phone with me checking on their progress. What a thrill ! The video was a huge hit with my boys. Miles was in middle school and Keaton was in the 3rd grade. They prioritized homework for about a solid week before surrendering to their old habits.

It was a great week and we still have Randy's video for family fun. You can see it on my YouTube page at :

https://www.youtube.com/
watch?v=NPjATHcg9xE&t=5s

* * *

A year before, a different Slim Jims spot called for an outdoors-type kid, rock climbing. We shot in the Sandia Mountains on the East edge of Albuquerque. Filming is seldom restricted to an eight-hour day. I had been working since dark thirty and I was whipped. At wrap time, I just wanted to go home. That was my excuse for speeding.

When the Sheriff's deputy pulled me over I was laughing at myself for being dumb. He asked what I was up to, where I was coming from and where I was going. I think he was assessing my demeanor, was I drunk? When I told him that I was returning from a film shoot he was curious – a commercial for what?

He lit up when I told him of Randy and the Slim Jims spot, saying that he watched wrestling with his son all the time and wished they could meet The Macho Man. But Randy was already on his way out of town.

Always looking for an angle, I asked if he'd like an autographed pic of Randy for his son. It was like I'd offered him a bag of gold. He was thrilled to get the picture, so I sweetened the deal with a few dozen Slim Jims from the shoot. He thanked me, told me to slow down, and kindly sent me on my way.

Was that a bribe? I think any judge would let it slide, if I gave them some Slim Jims, too.

CrimeStoppers

Of all the varied productions that I've worked on, crime scene re-enactments were the most fun. Cops are great to work with. They usually have a heart of gold and a dry sense of humor backed by an air of suspicion. My first was *CrimeStoppers*.

In 1977 Albuquerque Police Lt. Gregg MacAleese approached the local ABC affiliate to air crime scene re-enactments to entice the public to report suspicious activity related to crimes. It was the beginning of *CrimeStoppers*.

Gregg then contacted my mentor at UNM, Dr. Bob Hurtung, looking for students to act in the scenes and assist with props. Daddy Bob tagged me. For the first shoot they asked me to cast two actors in their late teens to play killers. That's all they told me, two guys kill a third 'friend.' I asked if they wanted an actor to play the dead guy and they declined. And they'd bring a gun so I didn't have to worry about that.

What they didn't tell me was that the scene was a party that ended in the murder. Three friends drink and smoke pot until the tables turn and one guy ends up dead in a trashy, dingy apartment with no furniture.

I arrived at the location with the two actors to meet the police. Filming was new to them and they were figuring it out on the spot. They decided to include a dead guy and I fit the bill with long, hippie hair and a sorry excuse for a beard. OK, I'll do it. As they set the scene they realized that they needed alcohol and pot – shit ! I told them that they should have alerted me and I would have prepared wine bottles filled with juice for the scene.

They were too focused on getting it done to listen to me, so they forged on, sending an officer to buy a six-pack and a couple bottles of wine at a store down the block. But what about pot ? We were three college theater students in 1977, of course we had pot, but we weren't dumb enough to whip it out in front of the cops, even if we were working with them. A crinkled cigarette stood in for a joint.

As the camera rolled we were directed to drink and start a scuffle over who's got the wine and who's bogarting the joint, until tensions rise and the shooting starts. We did seven takes, taking large sips of beer and wine each time.

When the police 'director' called wrap we were toasted. The officers got in their squad cars and took off, leaving three drunk college students to find their way home. And, to top it all off, they left the gun behind, a gun from their evidence room.

A few days later the story aired on the news. Viewers were asked to watch the re-enactment, hoping that it would jog a memory and lead to a call with a clue. The next day I was shopping at a local grocery store when I realized that I was being watched. A store manager and two shoppers cornered me. The manager told me that I should relax because he'd already called the cops. They thought that I was one of the killers. I tried to tell them that : A) I'm just an actor and, B) I WAS THE DEAD GUY !

APD officers arrived and cleared my good name.

* * *

Since its first chapter was formed in Albuquerque in 1976, CrimeStoppers USA programs have been responsible for more than six hundred thousand arrests, more than $4 billion in recovered property and over one hundred million in rewards paid out.

It Happened On Mulberry Street

Up until the 7th grade my family lived in Darby, Pennsylvania, one block outside the Philadelphia city limits. My grandparents lived a block away.

One evening my parents were out and Grammy was babysitting. I was young, maybe 4th grade. I talked Grammy into letting me watch TV before bed. There was a movie on. I remember that it was titled *It Happened on Mulberry Street*, but I may be mistaken.

The story started at a mortuary garage. A driver was preparing to deliver a body in a casket across town, but he was concerned that his hearing aid was on the fritz so he couldn't hear a thing. He drove off in the hearse anyway. As he approached a busy intersection, the story cut to a delivery truck driver approaching the same intersection with failing brakes. The truck driver blared his horn but the hearse driver couldn't hear.

The truck ran the red light and T-boned the hearse, causing it to roll, with the casket sliding out onto the street. As onlookers gathered, the lid of the casket opened and the corpse climbed out and ran down the street. Quite exciting for a nine-year-old. Emergency vehicles and cop cars raced to the crash scene.

About the same time I noticed police sirens in the distance in our town. As tension mounted on the screen, the local sirens got louder until it seemed they were coming down our street. My heart was racing and the police sirens were blaring, obviously getting very close. Were they chasing the dead guy on my very street ? My mind was spinning. I was way too young for my first heart attack.

Just then someone heavy clomped up our steps onto the porch and started banging on the front door. That was all I could take ! I tore ass up the stairs and hid under my bed, shivering in fright and screaming. Grammy rushed in and pulled me out into the room. She must have slapped me because I stopped screaming.

When I calmed down she told me that there was a fire at the end of our street and the police and fire trucks were racing to the scene. It was just my grandfather banging on the door, hoping to take me to see the trucks. Sweet Jesus ! I still avoid horror films.

Ted Bundy and OMI

In '81 I was asked to film a dozen autopsies. Yep, the real thing. The head Doc at Medical Investigators had an idea to solve crimes. The serial killer, Ted Bundy, had traveled from state to state, leaving unfortunate victims behind. He killed women in Washington, Oregon, Colorado and Utah. He was finally caught in Florida, but not until he'd committed another gruesome murder.

The Doc's idea was to create a national database for autopsies. Forensic details from crime scenes and autopsies would 'search' for matching details from active or cold cases nationwide when entered into the program. You've all seen Lennie Brisco* confer with forensic docs on *Law and Order.* It's very basic crime fighting.

We filmed bodies from varied tragedies, but the first case on the second week got to me. An 18-year-old girl was on the slab but there was no visible damage to her body. No gunshots, no slashing knife wounds, nothing.

So I asked the attending doc. The story was that she'd been killed by her boyfriend. He'd strangled her with the alarm clock cord. Yikes ! I nearly lost my lunch when he continued, detailing that it was an older clock with hands, so *THE TIME OF DEATH WAS ON THE CLOCK !* Call Alfred Hitchcock !

That last detail was too much for me, but I couldn't lose it in front of the docs. I raised the large video camera to my shoulder to hide behind and looked for a trash can to throw up. Across the room I saw a laundry basket. Bingo. I hustled over, took a few deep breaths, then cleared my throat and spit on the laundry a few times, still hiding behind the camera.

Luckily, I regained my composure, but I had an odd feeling that something was off. I looked back and realized that the laundry basket was filled with the murder evidence from another autopsy table, and I'd just spit all over it. YAAAAAAHHHHH! (quietly)

The case was a large man who had been stabbed in the back over a dozen times and I just spit all over his bloody, torn flannel shirt. Needless to say, I quietly slinked back to the first dead body and went on with the day. I told a cop about it twenty years later. He laughed.

Pink Shoes

Decades ago I worked at a Children's Psychiatric Hospital. I'm sad to say that most of the kids were there because their parents were nuts. Let's move past that. My supervisor was a tall blonde woman who had a thing for dressing in pink. She was strong and efficient, a great boss. She also loved to play basketball and wore a pink sweatsuit on the court. The men on the court would laugh at her, "You really think this chick in pink was any good," they'd chuckle. Then she blocked their shots and beat them all one-on-one. For the past many years I had worn red

Chuck Taylor high tops, but in her honor, I decided to switch to Pink.

I had just moved from New Mexico to the East Coast and drove north with my wife to visit friends in Freeport, Maine. One of the attractions in Freeport was an L.L. Bean outlet store that was open 24/7. What ? Could they possibly have customers at 3AM in this tiny town ? You betcha ! So we cruised over to shop in the wee hours. They had a wall of shelves filled with every color of Chuck Taylor's for women but only black and white for men. It was the mid '80s.

I approached a saleswoman and asked if they had any other colors for men. "What color," she asked. I replied "pink." She took a beat, folded her arms over her chest, and looked me up and down before announcing, "We don't sell pink shoes to men in Maine !" I wanted to reply "excuuuse me" all Steve Martin.

I found a different outlet and wore pink Chuck's for the next 20 years until my chiropractor made me switch to better shoes a few years ago. I still wear the pink Chuck's on occasion. They usually draw comments from strangers and that's the reason I wear them and other unusual clothes. They make people connect and smile. I'll wear them to a family wedding next week in, otherwise, formal attire.

About five years ago I added rental bowling shoes to my wardrobe – red, green and black with 9 1/2 on the heel. They always draw a comment and a smile from a new, momentary friend.

National Commercials – Southwest Productions

For ten years I served as assistant director at Southwest Productions. Owners Dave Roberts and Barry Kirk had it all going on, booking jobs for lots of national brands like Aleve, Slim Jims and numerous products for Procter and Gamble.

The Aleve account was fat. Most commercials are shot in a day or two but Aleve would book us for eight shoot days when they came, packaging four separate spots, shooting two days each. It was a challenge to prep for four locations shooting back-to-back. At the time, the Aleve campaign featured two workers, one with a headache, the other a helper, suggesting two Aleve tablets for relief.

We shot in thriving businesses which took a lot of pressure off the art department. Think of it: when we shot in The Man's Hat Shop we simply walked in, set some lights, and rolled the camera. No need to create interesting backgrounds since there were hundreds of hats of all kinds everywhere you looked.

I doubled as a location scout for many of our efforts and that led to some great interactions. One scenario was to be set in an art classroom. Remember high school ? Of course the teacher had a headache. I cruised to the Menaul School, founded in 1896. There was a kiosk with a security guard at the gate. He directed me to a large building behind administration.

The art classroom was huge, with a twenty-foot ceiling. The building was originally a sheep barn built around 1900. It was perfect. High ceilings and open floor plans help when setting lights and dolly tracks. I proceeded to the office to speak to the principal. She was very kind. She welcomed our production but seemed to hesitate. She humbly stated that we were welcome but she'd have to charge us a fee for our time on campus, $50 a day. If I had smiled any wider, my face would have cracked. I told her that we were prepared to pay $500 a day, both for prep and shoot days. She was quite pleased.

I returned with Dave, our director, to see the room and meet with the art teacher. Dave loved the room but wanted to make a few changes. The walls and ceiling were freshly painted, white, white, white. White is not conducive to filmmaking. It's too clean and reflective. There was a slop sink where the kids cleaned their brushes and that, too, had been scrubbed clean and the wall freshly painted white, looking unused.

Dave suggested that we paint the walls lavender and splash lots of different colors around the sink signifying the daily chores of the students. Dave scooted back to the office, leaving me to negotiate with the art teacher. That's when the shit hit the fan.

The teacher was proud of the room, clean and fresh in preparation for the coming school year. When I suggested that we repaint the room and splash paint on the walls he tensed up. I thought he might slug me. Time to dance. I told him that, after the shoot, we would return the room to the pure white walls as if we'd never been there. He settled down. Phewwww !

Our art department painted the room lavender and created a sloppy mess around the sink, splashing multi colors of paint on the wall and floor. Now it looked 'lived in,' like an active art classroom should. On the shoot day we moved in with twenty teens playing students and an actor portraying the stressed-out teacher. Production took over, setting lights and track to support the dolly on a tracking shot to open the commercial.

When we broke for lunch I invited the art teacher to join us. He hesitated, surveying his classroom, then came the surprise. With a huge smile, he told me he loved the way we'd changed his room and the happy colors. He told me not to have the room repainted. He loved it. He even wanted the color splashes around the sink left as they were. I think he realized that true, professional artists, had changed his environment for the better.

Thanks, Kylene and Mark !

* * *

During another series of Aleve ads, we travelled to Las Vegas, New Mexico, to shoot in a sort of new age castle at the Armand Hammer United World College. There are pics of the building on their website. The building had a vast ballroom with solid oak floors, perfect for a scenario involving two men refinishing the floor. The building was deemed unsafe at the time but somehow we were granted access.

In the early morning of our last day in Las Vegas, I got a call from the producer. She'd been unable to reach our key PA and she was concerned. I tried to reach him, to no avail, so we proceeded with the shoot, hoping that he would call. To preserve his privacy let's call the PA "Max".

We were scheduled to leave Las Vegas at the end of the day, returning to Albuquerque to continue the job. The next scenario featured a young rock climber practicing his skills in a climbing gym. Max was cast as the climber with a healthy boost in pay. As we packed to leave Las Vegas we got a distressing call. Max had driven back to Albuquerque the night before and had hung himself in his garage. Tragic. We were all in shock. He wasn't even 30 years old.

With the production wheels in motion for the eight-day shoot, it was determined that we had to press on. Numerous agency execs had flown in from New York as well as actors cast from LA. A local man was cast to replace Max.

Max was more than a work associate to me. He was my tennis partner and sought my advice on occasion, frustrated that he wasn't moving up the industry ladder as quickly as he'd hoped. That and relationship struggles had him on the ropes. I knew that he was stressed but had no clue that his depression had run so deep. I wasn't his counselor, just an older friend.

As AD, I ran the shoot. The art department had mocked up a climbing wall in a warehouse in town. The actor who replaced Max was ready and we started to shoot. I remember looking around at the crew. Everyone was crying silently as we muscled forward to complete the day. We all missed Max.

* * *

Some years later a close friend expressed a desire to kill himself. After talking for a while, I asked him to meet me at my home for coffee the next morning. Over coffee, he again mused that he'd be better off dead. I grabbed a few photos from my room and asked him to join me for a drive.

I drove him to the garage where Max had died. I shared pictures of Max and related to him the pain felt by myself and all of our company over Max's suicide. I'd been faced with suicide before and had come to the realization that, although suicide might relieve a person's pain, it would transfer that pain to their surviving family and friends. I'm happy to say that he chose to live on and now, twenty-some years later, he's thriving in a rewarding career.

* * *

Let's lighten the mood and go back to Las Vegas for another Aleve ad. This time the scenario was a bakery. We found a dilapidated storefront on the main drag and chose it as the location. The classic architecture and front bay windows were captivating. All it took was some paint on the exterior and lots of baked goodies displayed in the window.

We started in the early morning, dark thirty, on a cold, fall day. If you've never been to New Mexico you may have a vision of a vast, flat, hot desert. Not so. New Mexico is mountainous, with lots of forests and great skiing in Taos, Santa Fe, Los Alamos and more. Las Vegas itself is over 6,000 feet above sea level.

Our first shot was an exterior, a portrait of an age-old small-town business district. The "look" of the buildings was frozen in 1940. As is often the case, we chose to wet the street and sidewalks to give it all a fresh feel. Have you ever noticed wet streets in a film when there's no indication of rain ? It's for that clean look and the reflections off the wet surface. But we didn't cop to the reality of the chilly morning.

We'd contracted with the volunteer fire department to wet the area with their pumper truck and watched in horror as the street and sidewalk froze instantly, causing cars to slide and a store owner to slip and land on his butt. Luckily no cars crashed and the store owner was OK. Details !?!?

* * *

Years earlier I was hired to shoot a commercial for Kroger groceries in Las Vegas. Shot in the late '80s, it's still one of my favorite productions. The scene was the porch of a classic Victorian house. Two boys, six and four years old, are sitting on the stoop eating watermelon. The older boy pranks his brother telling him that he'd better spit out the seeds or a watermelon would grow in his belly. The little guy argued back – "will not" – "will too" – "will not."

They argued back and forth until a pregnant woman strolled by. Both boys spit out their seeds in a panic.

Pink Shoes and Formal Wear

I had a great time working for Dave and Barry at Southwest Productions. I served in a few crew positions as AD, production coordinator and location scout. On occasion, while serving as the AD, Dave would rush me into a costume to add a character to a shot.

A new office / shopping center was developed in the Santa Fe downtown area called The Lincoln Center and Southwest was hired to create their commercial. The thirty-second scene featured a *maître d'* in a tux welcoming guests to an upscale restaurant. Dave cast me as the *maître d'*. The tux was actually what's called 'morning tails.' You've seen men dressed in them during state funerals. The jacket is cut short at the waist with the tails extending to the back of the knee, very formal. Groucho Marx wore them, too, although rumpled as appropriate for his character. I was wearing classy black dress shoes to complete the look.

After a few takes the sound tech told Dave that my dress shoes were clicking on the hard surface creating a distraction. Everyone knew that I wore pink Chuck Taylor high tops and changing to them would solve the sound problem. Dave and Barry had a quick conversation. They determined that the frame was tight enough that they'd never see my feet, so I changed to my Chucks and we pressed on.

During the edit it was clear that the pink shoes were indeed in frame. What to do ? Momentary panic. It wasn't an option to re-shoot so, when the edit was complete, Dave met with the client, hoping that he wouldn't have an issue with my shoes. To our delight, he was elated. How perfectly Santa Fe for a formal *maître d'* to be wearing pink sneakers. The commercial was a hit !

* * *

We all know the phrase "It's not what you know, but who you know." While working on a feature film, running the production office, I got a call from Ann Lerner, a respected commercial producer. She told me that she'd heard that I was a good AD and wanted to hire me on a national commercial shooting in LA, with famed director Arnie Lerner. In fact, I'd worked on many sets but had never served as the AD (Assistant Director). It was a great opportunity so I accepted the gig and hopped a plane to LA.

The shoot was a huge Toyota spot with the set consuming an entire sound stage. There was no room to set up catering so we contracted for a second stage just to eat lunch. It was the sound stage for the show Soul Train, still set dressed with their logo and stage for their continuing production. How Fun !

That call from Ann rocketed my film career. The job of AD is a huge step up from production office coordinator. That was over 25 years ago and Ann is still a close friend. She went on to serve as Albuquerque's liaison to the film industry. She's also been instrumental as a consultant for this book.

Drugs and Rock 'n Roll

Long before jumping into the film biz I was just a crazy teen, smoking and selling lots of pot, and that led to some crazy times. I graduated high school in '69 and hadn't entered the hippie/drug culture yet. I attended a Jesuit college for my first year but was thrown out for protesting the war.

The University of Scranton was not a liberal school. While students across the country were staging sit-ins to protest the bombing of Cambodia, the students in Scranton were oblivious to the turmoil. There were only a dozen students willing to 'challenge' the administration to shut down for a day of protest.

The twelve of us decided to boycott our final exams, not real smart. Administration simply recorded failing grades in all of my subjects and tossed me out. My Mom held onto the expulsion letter and mailed it to me when I was in my late thirties. Thanks, Mom, you're such a kidder !

Back home I fell in with the 'wrong crowd,' to my delight. I entered the world of drugs and rock and roll. The drugs were mostly pot and hash with an occasional acid trip, and I sold pot to pay the bills. And the concerts were great: The Who, Traffic, The Grateful Dead. Great shows.

The cherry on top was *The Concert for Bangladesh* with George Harrison, Ringo, Eric Clapton, Leon Russell, Billie Preston and many more. Staged at Madison Square Garden, it was the first rock concert raising awareness and money for a cause, the starving people of Bangladesh, India. It was the first charity concert film, too. Check it out on YouTube.

*   *   *

One summer day I hitched to a friend's house to buy an ounce of pot but somehow he talked me into buying a kilo (2 1/2 lbs), and a dozen hits of LSD. I didn't want to walk around with that haul so I called my friend, John Dezio, and asked him to pick me up. John drove a sexy white and red Barracuda fastback. *Zoooooom !*

We were stopped in a cluster of cars, waiting for the light to change, when I decided to prank John. I told him that the ounce that I bought was rather heavy and opened the bag. He gasped when he saw the huge bundle.

At that moment ALL of the cars around us turned on their cop lights, placing those red flashing bubbles on their roofs, all unmarked cars. Oh, SHIT ! We started to panic. We were caught. We couldn't possibly throw the drugs out the window or attempt to eat it all. Who wants to eat two and a half pounds of pot ? We were over-the-moon nervous but just sat tight.

Lucky for us, the cops were after the guy in the car ahead of us. They directed us out of the cluster of cars and we were on our way. Phewwwwww !

* * *

A year or so later I was robbed, losing $700, my tuition for the next semester at a local college. I borrowed $200 from a friend, hoping to buy some pot to recoup the loss. A friend from work, Perkin's Pancake House, offered to introduce me to a dealer to recoup my loss. I was twenty years old and Leroy was in his early forties and a heroin addict. We headed to a rough neighborhood near downtown Philly.

Leroy pulled to the curb and motioned for a guy loitering on the sidewalk. As he approached I held my $200 out the window, expecting to trade it for the drugs. Once again, I was in the wrong place at the wrong time. We were suddenly surrounded by cop cars. The dude on the sidewalk grabbed my cash and ran.

The Philly cops took Leroy and me into custody. At the station they grilled me, made me strip naked and shoved me around a bit. But I had zero drugs, so I knew that I'd be OK. Not so for Leroy.

A week earlier I noticed that Leroy was wearing a small golden cross. When I asked about it he told me that a woman had cast a spell on him and the cross was part of a process to counter the spell. He told me that he wore the cross every day and had placed a dime in each sock. The idea was that the dimes would turn black when the spell was broken.

The cops had Leroy strip and you can imagine their disbelief as he tried to explain the reason for dimes in his socks. They completely lost interest in me and focused on Leroy, roughing him up as he tried to explain. Unbeknownst to me, Leroy was hoping to score as well. He had $400 bucks under the driver's seat which the cops 'confiscated.' We were both released since we didn't have any drugs.

Enough already. I had to get out of town. I stuck out my thumb and landed in Boston a day later.

From The Big Screen to
The Super Bowl

White Sands

The feature film *White Sands* was a colossal undertaking with big stars and a considerable budget, close to $30 million in 1990 dollars. The production suffered from delays in scheduling resulting in conflicts for the producers Scott Rudin and Bill Sackheim. By the time we were shooting they were both busy on other projects.

Adding to the confusion, our director, Roger Donaldson, was unfocused. He often started shoot days re-inventing the wheel, planning the shoot day on the morning of, even though he and the department heads had created efficient plans in prep. We had a tight budget for film stock, enough for our eleven-week shoot. But Roger's inefficiency caused us to shoot the entire film budget in the first three weeks. The studio wasn't happy.

Every day on a film production the office creates a 'production report.' It's a legal document detailing the cost of that day down to the tiniest detail; how much film was shot, how many pages of the script covered, who worked and for how many hours. The report is signed by the AD, the UPM, and the coordinator. At the top right corner of the report there's a tiny space where you declare whether you're ahead or behind schedule. Due to Roger's inefficiency, we were behind from the start, but I was instructed to lie daily, continually stating that we were on schedule.

After awhile the money folks in LA had had enough. They knew that we were behind. Roger bristled, saying that he was planning to cut some scenes and, thereby, be back on schedule. The end result was that the cuts created holes in the story leading to the *Rolling Stone* review calling the film : "A veritable shitstorm of incoherent inconsistencies."

* * *

The film's opening scene was complicated, with a camera mounted on the nose of a helicopter, flying through a canyon and elevating to reveal a dead body on the canyon rim of the Taos Gorge in Northern New Mexico.

There was a camera mount attached to the chopper, but it was old school, not like the mounts available today with 360-degree rotation. After completing the shot we shipped the mount to Ireland. Director Ron Howard needed it to film the opening sequence of his film *Far and Away* with Tom Cruise and Nicole Kidman.

Their opening shot was much like ours. The helicopter flew above crashing waves, revealing the lush, rolling hills on the Irish coast. But a mishap ruined their day. The pilot was flying low when a rogue wave smashed into the rocks sending a wall of water skyward. The chopper hit the ascending wave and stalled, dropping the bird into the water along with the pilot, camera operator, the camera and the mount. Fortunately, the men were rescued, but the chopper, the camera and the mount were lost. The mount was one of a kind and a replacement wouldn't be available for a year.

* * *

White Sands synopsis : A small-town sheriff finds a body in the desert along with a suitcase filled with $500,000. The sheriff impersonates the dead man and stumbles into an FBI investigation. Willem Dafoe played the Sheriff.

The climax of the film takes place at a military base at the White Sands National Monument in Southern New Mexico. We only needed a small section of a military base for the scenes so the art department and construction built a few small buildings in the tourist area of the monument. The White Sands National Monument comprises over 145,000 acres of white sand, gypsum, what they make plaster wallboard out of. The small buildings were easy to construct since all but one were empty shells. Only the base bathrooms had a finished interior where Mickey Rourke gets shot by Sam Jackson.

White Sands is near Alamogordo, New Mexico, and that's where we spent the last two weeks of production. To flesh out the base we needed military rolling stock, jeeps and trucks commonly seen on any base. But we were short on cash and couldn't afford to lease vehicles for the base.

So the art director sent a photographer to the New Mexico National Guard. They photographed jeeps and trucks, blew the photos up to life size and pasted the pictures on 4' x 8' sheets of plywood, then propped them up with 2x4s, creating a fake motor pool. Only one real jeep was on scene since it had to be driven. It worked ! The camera couldn't tell the difference.

God was on our side for a week and a half with great weather. On the day we wrapped the location a fierce wind destroyed the set but we were done and all was well. PHEWWWWWWW !

* * *

The last location on *White Sands* was a gas station on the road back to town, featuring Willem Dafoe and Mary Elizabeth Mastrantonio. As production office coordinator, I had planned a wrap party for that evening, complete with catering and lots of booze. The entire cast and crew were housed in hotels so no one would be driving. Efficient to a fault, I had everything planned by midday, so I drove to the gas station to watch the final scene.

After a bit I decided to drive back to the office. I had rolled a joint for the road and whipped it out as I left the location, sparking as I drove. Bad move. In less than a half mile I was pulled over by local cops – fuck! One of the cops questioned me as I sat in the driver's seat. He stumbled over himself, hinting that he 'smelled something', hoping that I'd confess. So I volunteered that, indeed, he was smelling that devil reefer. I got out of the car and handed him the joint. The other officer asked if they could search the car and I agreed, knowing that there was nothing else to find. We were about 30 minutes into their interrogation and search when the whole damn film crew drove past in a bus, waving as they passed.

NO ONE STOPPED TO RESCUE ME – THANKS A LOT – enjoy the party while I rot in jail.

But the incident ended on a positive note. After another uncomfortable fifteen minutes the officers told me that they'd let me go without a charge if I'd rip open the offending joint, sprinkle the pot on the ground, and dance on it. I happily obliged, keeping as straight a face as I could muster. I LOVE small town justice!

* * *

In fairness to Roger, I highly recommend two of his later films: *The World's Fastest Indian* starring Anthony Hopkins and *No Way Out* with Kevin Costner, Sean Young, and Gene Hackman.

The Fugitive

I didn't work on *The Fugitive*, that's not the point. It's great fun to see films made by friends that you worked with in the past. And, within the industry, there's great respect for our peers' efforts. *The Fugitive* was shot by Michael Chapman, nicknamed 'Chappie' on set. I worked with him on *Suspect Zero* and on another film that was never completed. Look up Chappie on IMDB. He was the DP on *Raging Bull*, *Taxi Driver* and *Primal Fear.* He was no slouch !

I saw *The Fugitive* in Crystal City, North of LA. The theater was packed. Towards the beginning of the story Harrison Ford is being transported in a sheriffs' bus, handcuffed and shackled along with other inmates. But a series of mishaps lands the bus in the path of an oncoming train.

The scene was shot on a stretch of the Smoky Mountain Railroad using the most practical special effects of all, a real train and a real bus. The movie was made before CGI effects became the standard in filmmaking, and instead of using miniatures the filmmakers simply placed a full-size bus in the path of an oncoming freight train and let the action do the rest. The bus was nearly torn in half by the impact, and the train was made to derail after the collision, leaving nothing but mangled wrecks in its wake. Fugitive Richard Kimble (Harrison) narrowly survives the destruction, going on to find the man who killed his wife.

I've seen many films in LA, a film industry town, and the audience often applauds at the end. But the train crash scene in *The Fugitive* was so dynamic that the entire audience jumped up and applauded at the end of the scene. There were lots of filmmakers in the audience. We're proud of our work.

I Went To Harvard

I went to Harvard, that is I landed in Cambridge, Mass. for a short time in 1972, so I strolled the gorgeous campus for kicks.

The week before I'd been dragged from a car by Philly Police and roughed up during questioning on a drug charge. I just wanted to get outta Dodge. I decided to hitchhike to Mexico, hoping to eat magic mushrooms with Carlos Castaneda in those crazy, hippie days.

I set out on a unique route to Mexico traveling North from Philly through New England to Boston, and continuing North to Canada. From there I'd travel thousands of miles to the West coast, then straight South through California to Mexico. It wasn't a well thought out plan.

My first night in Boston I slept at a Youth Hostel. In the morning, a fellow traveler asked me to join him in town at a quaint vegetarian restaurant he'd found. Sounded like fun. I'd been a line cook in pancake restaurants for a couple of years so a little mom and pop cafe would be a welcome change.

So we cruised to the Root One Cafe on Mass Ave (Massachusetts Ave) about a half mile from M.I.T. (Massachusetts Institute of Technology). It was a tiny, forty seat vegetarian cafe, three steps down from street level, with a large chalk board on the wall displaying their menu.

The food was great and as I ate I noticed a small message written in the lower right corner of the menu board. It read : *Interested in service through food, come join us.*

It turned out that the kitchen crew was a collection of young hippies, living together and running the cafe. I was intrigued… and I moved in that night. They had an apartment just off Harvard Square and an old farmhouse in West Roxbury. I chose the apartment for the first couple of weeks. It was a roach-infested dump but it was smack dab in the middle of a very exciting Cambridge neighborhood, bustling with entertainment and services for the well-heeled yuppie crowd.

Eventually I moved to the farmhouse in West Roxbury. It was about 200 years old and was the hub for a large farm operation back in the day, complete with a barn, a hayloft, and shelters for tractors and ploughs. But progress had eaten the land for housing developments over the decades and the farmhouse now sat on less than an acre.

Being in the farmhouse was the cherry on top. Fifteen or so random hippies, all 20 to 35, with a baby and two married couples, a true hippie commune with dreams of utopia and a true world family. It was a must that we were a sober community, no drugs or alcohol. Most of the group were studying New Age Spirituality.

One day a couple came in for lunch. After eating they came to the counter, thanked us for the great meal, and left us a tip, a brown bag full of peyote buttons. YOWWWWW !

How do you think our humble, sober, spiritual group handled it ? We hung a sign on the door that read 'Gone Fishin'. We closed for three days and took off to a lake house owned by somebody's parents.

We turned the windowless company van into a sauna, removing the seats and sitting cross-legged with hot rocks from the fire outside. It was another world.

Sam Jackson / Harrison Ford

November 1992 – I'm driving to Paramount Studios in LA.

I'd been invited to visit the set of the feature film *Patriot Games* by good friend Samuel L. Jackson. I'd recently worked with Sam on the film *White Sands*.

Patriot Games was a closed set but an experienced AD can charm their way past any hurdle, so I strolled to the shooting set. The big action scene at the end of *Patriot Games* has Harrison Ford piloting a speedboat followed by a foreign terrorist, the bad guy.

At Paramount there's a sunken section of the parking lot where they produced naval battle scenes with miniature ships following WWII. The depression was about three feet deep and, once filled with water and miniature battleships, it was any ocean and any naval battle.

The company was shooting Harrison's takes in a speedboat chase off the New England coast. It was a huge setup. Production added railroad tie walls to increase the depth of the pool, then added the tallest telephone poles I've ever seen, shooting upward from the pool. Huge silks were hung from the poles to simulate sky.

The DP had the electrics dept. set huge lights pointed up to the silks creating a moonlit scene of soft, bounced light. Harrison's speedboat was positioned in the middle of the pool, resting on a rocker arm that added movement to the boat, while the FX team splashed waves at the boat and blasted Harrison's hair with giant fans. WOW ! It was a gigantic setup !

Between shots I approached an AD looking for Sam. I was crestfallen when he told me that Sam wasn't on set that day. Damn. I walked away sulking like Charlie Brown after getting tricked by Lucy.

But someone called my name. It was an FX crew member from *White Sands*. He said that he was busy but wanted me to stay so we could catch up. He motioned to a set of three director's chairs facing a set of monitors and asked me to take a seat and wait for him.

I sat in the middle chair. The monitors were blank, but a moment later Harrison Ford sat in the chair to my left and director Phillip Noyce sat to my right, greeting me as they landed. There was no question of who I was. I was on the set so I must belong. Together we watched the clips from the last couple of 'takes.'

I CAN DO THIS! I can survive the long hours, the weeks away from my kids, the cold nights and blazing noons on set…. I can do this. The magic moments are worth it !

* * *

I call Sam Jackson a 'good friend,' let me explain. In TV and film production you meet and collaborate on countless projects with new set friends, a new crew and list of actors for each production, and you get close for the length of the project, for a couple of days to many months, then you never see them again. And they're your friend, a set friend.

I count Bryan Cranston, Mary Elizabeth Mastrantonio, Victoria Principal and Billy Crystal as good friends but they wouldn't know me today without an introduction.

Samuel L. Jackson

On set Mr. Jackson was known as Sam. It was 1992 and Sam wasn't a big star yet. He served for 12 weeks as our "cover set" actor.

A cover set is an indoor set prepared for a last-minute change in schedule due to weather. Production had rented an entire motel in Taos, New Mexico, with plenty of rooms for all cast and crew, and five rooms converted into production offices.

A room a few doors down from the production coordinator's office, my office, was decorated to play Sam's FBI office. It was dressed on our first day in Taos to be ready for any weather event. Sam hung around a lot, waiting for his scenes to be scheduled.

Since the crew was off on location during the day, Sam often hung out with us in the office. I was blessed to spend long hours with him, chatting while doing office work to support the show.

He spoke of his family, his wonderful wife, LaTanya, who had stuck with him during his early struggles with substance abuse. He was grateful for her support and for the opportunities afforded him. That was 1992.

In the 'small world' category, in 2022 *People* magazine featured Sam and La Tanya as their cover story, recounting the strength of their commitment to one another and Sam's redemption from addiction. Sam told me the whole story 30 years previous over coffee. What a privilege.

I celebrated my 40th birthday on the shoot in Taos. The Assistant Coordinator, Jilann Spitzmiller, planned a group dinner for my birthday at a lovely restaurant. Sam and actor M. Emmett Walsh* joined the dinner and we had a roaring good time. I've often stretched the truth saying that Sam hosted my birthday party. Anyone who knows me knows that I embellish on occasion. They know that I'm full of baloney, but it's fresh, American-made baloney, and truly good for you.

Willem Dafoe

Willem was also cast in *White Sands*. Since he was one of the A-list stars, he was usually away shooting during the day. But when he was off, he'd spend hours on end practicing his fly fishing, casting on the spacious lawn across from our office. It was fun to watch him while making dozens of phone calls.

Stars are often granted assistants and Willem requested one. Usually actors are driven to set by a union driver, Teamsters, but for some reason Willem asked that his assistant double as his driver. My assistant, Jilann, had a boyfriend, Hank Rogerson, who'd hoped to score a job as a camera assistant, but there was no salary for another camera position. So I hired Hank as Willem's assistant. Willem was very kind. He only asked Hank to drive him, not to run menial chores for him during the day. So Hank drove Willem to the set each day and volunteered to assist in the camera dept.

Hank and Jilann went on to brilliant careers as documentary filmmakers. They were married sometime later. They worked together on award-winning documentaries and established a company called DocuMentors to help aspiring documentary filmmakers find their confidence in the art of documentary filmmaking. Look up DocuMentors online and both Hank and Jilann on IMDB.

At the end of production Willem came to my office and gifted me his character's Ray Ban Aviator sunglasses. What a sweetheart !

David Wisnievitz

I'd be remiss if I didn't send a shout-out to the UPM, Unit Production Manager on *White Sands*, David Wisnievitz. David was a great boss, always supportive and kind. During production my family suffered a tragic loss. Two carfuls of family members were involved in a tragic accident in Eldorado, New Mexico, near Santa Fe, when a road collapsed in a rainstorm, killing my Sister-In-Law, Patti.

After spending the night comforting family at St. Vincent's Hospital, I reported to the office to bury myself in work. But David noticed that I was distraught and weary from crying. When I recounted the tragedy to him, including the fact that two family cars had been wrecked, he told me to take a fifteen-passenger van to help with our family and to return to work when I was ready. Incredibly generous.

I was gone for more than a week. It was a tough time for the family. Jilann took on my work as well as her own while I was away, easily doubling her responsibilities. What a blessing, to work with saintly associates like David and Jilann.

Mary Elizabeth Mastrantonio

A little background first : when I married my love, Johanna, I took her name, hyphenating, so my new moniker was Charlie Johnson-O'Dowd.

On the film *City Slickers* I was listed in the credits as Assistant Production Coordinator. In fact I was the coordinator but another crew member threatened to sue if she didn't get that credit. No sweat.

But when my sister, Sharyn, saw the film in a theater she decided to poke some fun. She called, remarking that my credit was so long that it stretched across the screen. She went on, joking that I'd have to avoid working with Mary Elizabeth Mastrantonio because her credit would be longer. That week Mary Elizabeth was cast in the film *White Sands,* and I was the production coordinator. I told Mary Elizabeth the story when I met her and, in true Hollywood style, she returned the next day with an autographed headshot for my sister. It reads : 'Dear Sharyn, I win! Ha Ha Ha Ha Ha' followed by her flowing signature.

I highly recommend a film Mary Elizabeth starred in with Kevin Kline, Susan Sarandon, Rod Steiger, Harvey Keitel and Alan Rickman entitled The January Man, directed by her husband, Pat O'Conner.

Mickey Rourke – YIKES !

Mickey Rourke was cast as a bad guy in *White Sands*. He was a bad guy in real life, too. Mickey was playing a government agent but he insisted that his wardrobe come from an exclusive LA tailor, Tyler Trafficante. That made no sense since government agents probably buy their suits at Sears. In addition, Mickey's character gets shot in the film, meaning that we'd need multiple sets of the costume he was shot in for additional takes. OK, it's not in the budget but we'll figure it out. The producers granted his request.

The costume designer asked me to contact Mickey's management and secure a date when she could meet him to choose his wardrobe. Mickey responded that he would choose his wardrobe by himself. It took some negotiating, but Mickey finally agreed that she could be there, but only to observe !?

We had $15,000 in the budget for his entire wardrobe but he spent $75,000 in one day. His socks cost $75 a pair in 1990 dollars. At the conclusion of the shoot he walked away with more than half his wardrobe without asking.

* * *

Mickey traveled with an entourage. His circus train consisted of his personal trailer, a tricked-out bus owned by Sylvester Stallone and rented for the shoot, followed by a

40-foot semi-trailer equipped with a full gym that he never used, followed by an antique pickup truck and two Harleys ridden by his associates. Try fitting that ensemble on the tiny Santa Fe streets when shooting on location.

* * *

I was tight with a few realtors in Santa Fe and found a luxury home for Mickey. The agents also found me a great home for Sam Jackson. Sam was stoked since he was only approved for a hotel room since he wasn't a major star yet. I was able to get the home for a bargain that fit in the budget. The home meant that his family could stay with him during the twelve weeks of production. Sam was very appreciative.

I don't remember how it happened but I ended up surrendering the second home for Mickey's entourage and Sam had to make do with a hotel room. Mickey pulled rank and the producers caved.

* * *

After wrap I asked the producer why he'd tolerated Mickey's shenanigans. The role was originally offered to Ed Harris, but for whatever reason, he passed. The producer responded that Mickey was the biggest American star in the European market since Jerry Lewis and the overseas box office would recoup the entire budget.

Cheyney State

Twenty years old and without a car, hitchhiking was my regular mode of transportation. It led to many interesting conversations. One day a college professor picked me up. He taught philosophy at Cheyney State, a historically Black College (HBCU) outside Philly. We had a great chat and he invited me to attend his classes. So I applied, was accepted, and moved into the dorms, a unique experience.

During the day there were numerous white students in attendance, but there were just five white men in the dorms, and no white women. The experience of being a white man, but a distinct minority in that situation, was a lesson every white person should experience. I dove headlong into the experience while the other four white guys stayed in their rooms.

Most of the black students were gracious and friendly but there were a few who simply didn't want me there, a situation turned on its head. I was experiencing discrimination like many of them experienced constantly in their lives.

* * *

My parents lived about a half hour away so, on a weekday evening, I invited four friends to join me on a drive home to pick up 'school supplies' (pot, of course).

My parents lived in Sharon Hill which, at the time, was an exclusively white suburb. It's integrated now.

When we pulled up to the house I asked the guys to wait while I went in to see if it was OK for them to come in. I returned to them quickly and invited them in. My mom and three of my sisters were quite gracious, as we always were to all people. After a short chat we got back in the car to head back to school.

In the car, the guys were quiet. I asked what was up and one of them mentioned that he'd never been in a white household before. They all said the same. It turns out that they thought that I'd gone in to ask my parents if black guys were allowed in our house. It was 1971 and I assure you that they didn't say 'black guys.'

I laughed my ass off, telling them that I had four sisters and there was usually at least one of them running around in their underwear. I had just gone in to see that everyone was decently clothed. They cracked up and related that they were blown away that they were welcomed in a white home and double blown away that my older sister sat on the couch, breastfeeding, while chatting with them.

As crazy as that seemed I realized that I'd never been in a black family's home either. Living now in Virginia Beach, I partner with many black friends on projects generated at our church. And we're welcome in each other's homes.

Fight Night – Sports TV

In 1987, the Federal Government confirmed the right of Tribal governments to operate casinos on tribal lands, but New Mexico balked, delaying approval until 1995. Then they exploded. Nineteen pueblos played their hands, opening casinos of varied sizes all over the state. I presume there are even more now.

Albuquerque is surrounded by tribal lands. Huge casinos opened in every direction – Sandia Casino to the North, Isleta to the South, and Acoma Sky City to the West. Santa Ana Star Casino, North in Bernalillo, soon followed. I'm not a fan of legalized gambling but the casinos generated capital for the tribes and new opportunities for film crews. Every casino needed commercials. And they added entertainment to draw the crowds.

Sandia hosted televised boxing matches and Santa Ana Star competed by hosting *King of the Cage* matches. They were brutal. I served as the floor director, sitting ringside with the show's announcers. The producer and director are in a production trailer nearby but their only view is whatever the cameras see. As the floor director I was connected to them by headset, filling in anything that they can't see and 'babysitting' the on-air talent.

We were situated at the lip of the ring. I could reach across our table and touch the ropes. I always dressed in a nice shirt and tie and almost always left with at least a few drops of blood on the shirt.

At one match the 'color' announcer was famed boxing trainer Teddy Atlas. For every televised sport there's a pair of announcers, the 'play-by-play announcer,' calling the action and the 'color' announcer commenting on the athlete's background and such. I sat next to Teddy.

Teddy Atlas was a trainer. Online somebody wrote that "Atlas has trained a plethora of pugilists"? English please?! Teddy isn't a big guy but a long scar on his face suggests a tough guy attitude from his early life. His face was slashed in a street fight requiring 400 stitches, ouch squared!

Teddy's a sweetheart, kind and generous. My son, Keaton, came to the event, sitting by my side. He was 13. His older brother, Miles, was 17. He worked the boom pole, dangling a mic over the ring to record the announcer.

Prior to the broadcast, Keaton roamed the stands filled with rabid fight fans. He noticed a commotion and had to explore. There was a VIP seating area separated from the crowd by a security railing. A pile of fans were hanging over the railing, waving hats and T-shirts to a VIP. It was boxing great Sugar Ray Leonard in the front row, and the fans wanted an autograph.

Always the helper, Keaton sprang into action, taking hats and T-shirts from the fans, one at a time, for Sugar Ray to sign. That went on for fifteen minutes. I cracked up and commented to Teddy that my son was Sugar Ray's bitch. He's now a six-foot-six Marine Staff Sergeant and nobody's bitch.

Keaton and Ossian Shorr O'Dowd

At the end of any fight there's still airtime to fill and a final wrap up. Keaton was sitting with me during the wrap-up and noticed that Teddy sported an enormous ring, a championship ring of some kind, encrusted with diamonds so imposing that it would embarrass Elizabeth Taylor. At the end of the broadcast, he asked Teddy about the ring. Teddy took off the ring and slid it onto Keaton's hand. I remember that he slid it onto his skinny finger and it fell off into his hand to smiles all around. It was the cherry on top of a memorable event.

* * *

Last night I told Keaton that I'd written an account of that night. He cracked up and told me that when the ring dropped into his hand he had a wild thought. If he could get away with the ring he could sell it and buy the family a mansion !? He was 13. He scanned the area, looking for an unguarded exit but chilled and handed the ring back to Teddy.

* * *

Boxing is a brutal sport but nothing compared to *King of the Cage*. A cage match is fought in a boxing ring but the ropes are gone, replaced by a chain link fence, no escape.

I only worked one cage match, that was enough. Again, I sat with the on-air talent ringside. Prior to the fight the announcers commented that one of the fighters had been released from prison recently, prison, not jail, and he had a score to settle. The bell rang and the fight was on.

The ex-prisoner charged his opponent, knocking him to the mat right in front of us. He grabbed his opponent's hair and raked his face along the chain link fence only a few feet from us. The poor fighter was close enough to hear the color announcer blab on the air about the grudge the former prisoner was working off by beating him senseless. Holy Shit !

I can't imagine how defeated he felt. He lost the fight and I had lots of blood on my shirt.

Public Safety Ad – Like A Blue Movie

When Bill Richardson ran for Governor of New Mexico in 2002 he had the support of the IATSE film union. You've seen the IATSE logo in the credits of most feature films. IATSE – International Association of Theater and Stage Employees.

Once elected, he wanted to have a hand in any videos produced by State agencies. He asked the IATSE business agent to recommend a director and I got the call. That led to five years of videos produced about health, safety, DWI, handicapped parking, identity theft, and tourism. The Governor appeared in some of the spots. He was quite friendly and gave me a nickname, pink shoes. I wore pink Chuck Taylor high tops for twenty-plus years until my chiropractor insisted that I wear shoes with better support.

When the state added the installation of breathalyzers in cars following a DWI arrest, I was asked to create a PSA. I wrote a pretty good script and was ready to shoot when I got a call from the Dept. of Transportation. The executive said that he liked the script but wanted to change the final line. In the story a man picks up a date and has to blow into the breathalyzer to start his car. The date continues from dinner to an amusement park and finally to dancing, all in thirty seconds. Each time he has to use the breathalyzer to start the car and the young lady takes offense, walking away and making a hand gesture signifying 'loser.'

The exec insisted that I drive to Santa Fe to meet in his office to discuss changing the ending of the spot. The head of the safety campaigns for the state would be there as well. She was always supportive, so I drove the 60 miles, went to his office and sat across from his desk, awaiting the big news. He first mansplained that the point of the commercial was the breathalyzer. No shit. He dragged out his presentation until, finally, he suggested that the final line should be, wait for it, "Don't drink and drive or you may end up blowing more than your date." Honest to God !

I laughed and told him that no actor would say that line. He bristled and shot back "The Governor will say that line ! " Again, I said that there was no way that the Governor would say the line. He was pissed and told me that his decision was final. That I HAD TO shoot it that way. I left, shaking my head and rolling my eyes. Word in Santa Fe must have spread fast because I got a cell call halfway back to Albuquerque.

I knew that it was the Governor's office because the caller asked, "Is this Pink Shoes ?" It was the Governor's aide. He told me to postpone the shoot and attend a meeting with the Governor the next day. When I showed up, the Gov was absent but a dozen execs were seated around a large round table in the conference room. I was instructed to scrap the new line and shoot the spot as I'd written it.

The Transpo exec looked deflated. None of the execs at the table addressed him and his idea. They approached the issue head-on with no debate.

Sadly, politics took over and the Transpo exec screwed me. He contracted with production companies in Texas and California to produce the public safety ads that I'd been shooting for five years. Time to scare up some other work to pay the bills.

My replacements made a few mistakes. My favorite was an ad for New Mexico Tourism shot on a road featuring fake Saguaro cactus, neglecting the fact that Saguaro cactus only grow in Arizona.

A Texas company filmed an ad with an all-white cast for services in New Mexico. New Mexico is a Hispanic majority state ! It's customary to follow *West Side Story* rules – whites and Hispanics together. An all-white cast in NM is a sure flop.

Super Bowl Commercials –
Sierra Mist & Coke

In 2003 an ad agency produced a Super Bowl commercial for Sierra Mist. The spot tracked monkeys in the zoo, sweltering on a hot day. To cool off, the monkeys construct a seesaw to propel each other into the cold pool in the polar bear enclosure next door. Fun concept.

Researching zoos around the US, the agency decided to shoot at the Rio Grande Zoo in Albuquerque. I was tagged to co-produce the scene. The first half of the spot with live monkeys, and all post-production, were done in LA, but the zoo entrance and the polar bear exhibit were ours to complete. Of course, the monkey in our shots was a dummy dropped from a huge construction crane hovering above.

The DP was Janusz Kaminski who shot *Schindler's List* and *Saving Private Ryan* for Steven Spielberg. It was an honor to work with him.

For the initial shot Janusz instructed the grips and camera department to position the camera just above the water line looking up at the polar bears, the POV* of the monkey cooling off in the water. They employed a jib arm* to reach into the exhibit over the stone and glass wall protecting zoo visitors. In every location I communicate with a facility manager on site to protect us from ourselves. The zoo was a unique location and there may be hazards or policies that we were unaware of.

Once the camera was mounted, the grips swung the jib arm into the enclosure. We were ready to shoot. Then I got a tap on the shoulder. It was the zookeeper. He asked me to look at the polar bear and asked, "Do you see what the polar bear is looking at ?" Sure, I responded, he's looking at the camera. That's the shot we want, like he's looking at the monkey in his pool.

"No," he said, "the polar bear is looking at that long crane arm and wondering if he can jump on it and climb out of the enclosure and eat your crew." We re-positioned the camera !

The commercial is online, posted by the Hall of Advertising. Both of my sons are in the commercial as young zoo visitors.

* * *

In 1990 I was in LA working for Eggers films. The job was a Super Bowl commercial for Coke. It was a massive undertaking. The plan was to shoot the spot as if it was live at halftime. But we had to shoot the spot before we knew what teams would be playing. To cover all possibilities, we had the teams outfitted in varied colors, hoping to match the eventual contestants.

There were tons of extras. A college marching band was on the field and at least 500 fans in the stands. Actor Leslie Nielsen* was in the crowd, ready to deliver some comic lines. Director Bob Eggers gave me my first huge assignment. I was just a PA but was 40 years old and a loud clown. Bob had me direct the crowd of fans and he directed Leslie, 500 to one !

Then the Gulf War started and we got scammed by a little corporate espionage. Pepsi leaked to the press that they would forego their Super Bowl commercial in respect for our troops, saying that they would use the airtime to support the war effort. Coke decided to follow suit, electing to replace our commercial with a supporting message as well, shelving the spot that cost at least a million bucks in early '90s dollars.

On game day, Pepsi ran their comic ad, and Coke ran the disclaimer. We were totally scammed ! Our Coke ad was shelved since it was made to look like it was live at halftime and would seem dumb if broadcast after the game.

Miles – My Oldest Son

Miles was a great son, always chipper, always helping. He worked on some commercials with me but he had a passion for live theater. He earned a theater degree from UNM, alma mater of his mom and myself.

Miles was quite talented. When he was in high school a director friend exclaimed that he had fabulous stage presence, you just wanted to look at him. He was also skilled in stage fighting, having earned a junior black belt at 15. His fighting skills served him well as a swordsman in a production of *Romeo and Juliet*.

He was first cast in a high school production following the life of the Russian activist Leo Trotsky. Miles played Trotsky. Knowing that this was his first performance, his mother and I offered to 'run lines' with him, helping him to memorize his part. He declined. At the performance, to our amazement, he knew his part backwards and forwards, and even assisted his female counterpart when she forgot her lines.

Miles was equal parts sage and clown.

At UNM, Miles took classes in acting and directing. In one class he directed a short play and asked me to attend the in-class performance. The scene was well played but afterwards he noted that the cast had rushed the performance, shaving ten seconds off the running time. Ten seconds ? His attention to detail was spot on.

Outside UNM he was cast in a re-imagining of *A Streetcar Named Desire* produced by the local Tricklock Theater Company. The Tricklock crew were arguably the best community theater group in town. The play was an ambitious undertaking and Miles fit perfectly with the cast of older and more experienced actors. Over the years, I cast Tricklock actors in regional commercials and hired three of them to direct plays that I produced at UNM. Tricklock disbanded a few years ago.

In his final play at UNM Miles was cast as a complicated character, half man, half centaur. Numerous times in the play he had to drive his fists into the stage and kick his heels towards the ceiling. He was acrobatic and amazing but he overdid it, needing six months to recover from the physical stress.

* * *

Due to my contentious divorce, Miles and Keaton went separate ways. Keaton lived with me in town and Miles stayed with his mother, isolated in the East mountains. In his mid-twenties he rejected school and work, drinking and playing video games for three years. His mother was suffering with cancer but continued to work as a therapist in town.

Miles took her death very hard. I believe that he wanted to be her savior but there was nothing he could do. Her death weighed heavy on him, about twelve years ago. Once she passed he moved into town but never really got on track, drinking heavily and working jobs below his skills and intelligence. He had earned a BA in Theater Arts but continued to isolate, only performing in two plays in his last seven years.

He remained close to his mother's family and I know that it was a great comfort for him.

Sadly, Miles passed away at thirty-six years old, Thanksgiving week of 2022, a victim of depression and alcohol abuse. His friends and family praised him at a memorial service on his birthday in February 2023.

We Miss you, Miles !!!

Miles' On-Screen Debut

Although Miles appeared in a few commercials and short films, he was first on camera before he could give his OK.

He was delivered by a midwife in a birthing center in Bethesda, Maryland, February 26, 1986. The center was a house repurposed as a birthing center, with births in individual bedrooms, very cozy.

Johanna and I whiled away the time at home, waiting to leave for the center. We were propped up in bed watching live music performances on the Grammy Awards telecast. To our surprise, Miles Davis played and received a lifetime achievement award. We had already decided to name Miles after the famed trumpeter. It was a sign.

* * *

When he was four weeks old we returned to the center for a follow-up visit. We were greeted by a local reporter filming a story about midwives for the local news. They filmed Miles and Johanna for the story and used many shots of them during the reporter's voiceover. The final moments of the story focused on Johanna holding Miles as the reporter proclaims that "the practice of midwives was as old as Miles was young." I wish I had asked for a copy of the story.

Miles Memories

After our divorce, Johanna moved with the boys to Louisville, Colorado, a lily-white suburb outside Boulder, for two years. I moved to LA to try to solidify my film career. The first time the boys visited me they flew as unaccompanied minors. Keaton was five and Miles was nine. The pilot walked them up the ramp towards me. I was excited to see them and anxiously waved. Always the kidder, Miles turned to the pilot and quietly declared "I don't know that man." I have eagle ears, so I heard him. The cautious pilot was nervous but he checked my ID and rolled his eyes as Miles hugged me and laughed. Little booger !

* * *

One night, after Johanna and boys moved back to Albuquerque, Miles snuck out of the house to join a friend around midnight. They walked to Jefferson Middle School where they were in the seventh grade together. It was just two blocks away, in the neighborhood. For whatever reason, they were armed with a bat. The school was under renovation and the construction workers had failed to secure the building, leaving a door wide open. The boys couldn't resist. They entered the school and proceeded to the teacher's lounge where they smashed the glass out of a vending machine and stuffed their pockets with candy.

What they didn't realize was that they had tripped a silent alarm when they entered, alerting the school district security. Munching on candy bars, they headed for the open door only to be surprised by a security officer. They ran and somehow found a ladder leading to the roof. I never heard how the guard got them down.

The phone startled me out of my sleep. School security informed me that the boys had been turned over to the Albuquerque Police and were downtown in a holding cell. I picked Miles up in the early morning and took him directly to the school. I surrendered him to the principal who was on the lookout for the boys. She escorted us to the teacher's lounge to survey the damage to the vending machine. There was a tag on the machine with a phone number for the vendor.

When we got home, about 9AM, I called the vendor to take responsibility for the broken glass and stolen candy. He was taken by surprise. He told me that this was the first time anyone had ever copped to vandalizing one of his machines, and was double surprised since he hadn't yet heard of the damage from the school.

Miles' mother and I were divorced but we both showed up for his court date. The judge was surprised, saying she seldom saw a single parent supporting their kid, let alone a pair of divorced parents. She admonished Miles and sentenced him to community service.

At school the principal tacked on two weeks assisting the janitor after classes.

* * *

I grew up with four sisters, my mom and two grandmas, and never learned to fight. Dad always worked two jobs to keep us afloat, so the female energy was prevalent. Facing that reality, I enrolled Miles and Keaton in karate classes, wanting them to have the skills and courage to protect themselves. Their teachers were fantastic and they worked hard at it, earning Junior Black Belts in their teens.

Miles had a collection of swords that I'd gifted him over the years. They were replicas and not very sharp but they were heavy and looked impressive. He would practice choreographing fighting moves with them on the lawn, a born actor. He loved to scare the hell out of me, backing me against a wall as he swung a sword, menacingly. I learned to stay very still as he'd swing his sword and stop only an inch from my nose, wearing a shit-eating grin. He never hit me. I'm still amazed at his control.

Reality vs. Reality TV

Cowboy U

Cowboy U was a reality show produced for MTV. The idea was to take eight contestants from their city life, pluck them down on a ranch, and abuse the crap out of them. The last contestant standing won $25,000.

It's the only reality show that I worked on, serving as AD for two seasons. The best part of the show was the locations, first on the tiny Hawaiian island of Molokai, where the leper colony was founded and still exists, and the second time high in the Rockies outside of Cripple Creek, Colorado. Heavenly !

In the film biz your reputation is everything. I got a call out of the blue from a director that I'd worked with for a week ten years previous, shooting Spanish-language Ford truck commercials on Ghost Ranch. David Wechter had already completed a few seasons on the show, but they were heading for Hawaii and needed to replace their AD. It took me less than a split second to say yes.

David apologized that there were limited rooms in the only hotel on the island and asked if I'd consider living in a tentalow on the beach. A tentalow is a canvas tent built on a wooden platform with a private shower and commode. Twist my arm ! I'm livin' on the beach in Hawaii and getting paid.

The show shot in two shifts, with cameras following the contestants from dark thirty to past sundown. I ran the second shift and partied on the beach every night into the wee hours with the other crew members, also housed in tentalows, playing music on the beach around roaring fires.

When I first arrived on Molokai I went directly to the ranch where I found the lead cowboy, Rocco, sitting astride his horse in the middle of the rodeo arena with a local Hawaiian, Uncle Billy. Rocco's a big man. He runs a ranch in Scottsdale, Arizona, with his wife, Laurie.

Cowboy U was a series of competitions run by Rocco and his sidekick. It was real cowboy stuff with some crazy events sprinkled in. There were four married couples competing. There was riding and roping, shooting, both from a standing position and while riding a horse, driving a chuckwagon team, and herding cattle.

One crazy event had the four men sitting in a corral on cheap Walmart plastic deck chairs. Then we released a bull into the corral. The last man to run away won the event. It sounds brutal, but nobody was hurt. One contestant tried to scale the corral fence but slipped and fell, coiling into a fetal position on the ground as the bull rammed him repeatedly. The bull's horns were clipped and the contestant escaped with minor bruises. The deck chairs were trashed, but the contestants survived. Plus, there was always a medic on hand.

The morning crew pulled pranks like releasing squealing pigs into the dorms at 5AM, scaring the wits out of the women.

Reality show contestants are a different breed altogether. A few of them had stars in their eyes, thinking that their appearance on the show would rocket them to an acting career. Think again !

To dramatize the remoteness of the island we put contestants in a small boat, sent them out into the ocean, then rolled the camera and cued them to come to the shore. Rocco greeted them when they arrived on the beach. My favorite couple landed on the beach and got out of the boat. The wife of the pair was standing in shallow water when she turned to Rocco and asked how high they were above sea level !? Really !

She didn't win. Her husband was a character, too. He claimed adherence to a primitive spiritual path, sleeping on a bed of sharp stones that he arranged on his bunk each night.

* * *

There was a lovely couple from Philadelphia, the only black contestants in my two seasons on the show.

One evening the producer came to me with an issue. She thought that she smelled pot on the breath of the Philly couple. I confronted them gently, not wanting to cause a stir. After a short time, the husband lifted his foot revealing what was left of a joint. He told me the name of the local that supplied them. The next day I approached the dude, making it very clear that he was not allowed to give pot to the cast. But the crew was a different story. He partied on the beach with us every night for the next week.

We partied hard. I never woke before 10AM. One morning I was sound asleep when my cell phone rang. You know that panic: the phone rings in the middle of the night, somebody must be dead. I leapt out of bed but caught my foot in the sheets and fell, wrenching my knee. Ouch. I would need help walking. Does anybody have a set of crutches lying around ?

Within an hour the art director made me a cane out of 1 X 2 pine. It was the right height with a comfortable handle. On the side he had inscribed 'Bubba's Magic Leg.' It was an incredible act of love. I'll never get rid of that cane.

The Philly couple won the 25 grand.

* * *

For me, the immersion in the local culture and a strong friendship with Rocco were keys to the experience. Molokai is a tiny island with just one main road down the middle.

Local families had lived there for generations. Everybody knew everybody else and treated each other like family. Elder men were called 'uncle', a term of honor and respect. Uncle Billy was always with us, the clear leader of the clan. As AD on the show, I seem to outsiders be the one in charge, always louder and more visible than the director. After a week the locals called me Uncle Charlie. I felt honored.

* * *

As part of the show each season the cast was treated to a sit-down dinner featuring local cuisine. The art department fancied up a long picnic table and the cast arrived, happy to finally have something civilized to do. Of course the dinner was on camera. The menu consisted of two main dishes, poi and Rocky Mountain Oysters. Poi is a traditional staple food in the Polynesian diet, made from smashed taro root – it's like eating Elmer's glue, so the group chowed down on the oysters, lightly breaded and fried. That is until Rocco explained that Rocky Mountain Oysters are sliced bull's testicles, breaded and deep-fried. You can imagine the reaction. We served them again in Colorado so I had to give them a try. They were delicious, tasting like thinly sliced, breaded eggplant. Yummm – balls !?

* * *

My second season on the show was in Cripple Creek, Colorado. Let me explain a 'season' in film industry parlance. A season comprises a set number of episodes. The filmmakers gather for however long it takes to complete them. In the case of *Cowboy U* it took a month to shoot a season. Then the crew moves on to another production until they're called back to shoot the next season, if they're available.

* * *

I've always loved the band called The Band* and their rendition of the song "Up On Cripple Creek", so traveling to this tiny mining town felt special. The ranch that we'd be shooting on was about a half hour away from the town. On a few occasions I had to stop for a herd of elk slowly crossing the road.

The town is tiny and quiet, well suited to vacationers exploring the remnants of a coal mining past long gone. When I checked into the hotel the clerk mentioned that there would be an art show on the weekend. I remember that I rolled my eyes, scoffing at the idea of an art show in this podunk town. After all, I'm a filmmaker from the big city. Boy, was I wrong. The art and artists were amazing. I bought seven pen and ink drawings from one talented local artist, Jon Zimmer, some for myself and some to gift to family and friends.

* * *

Much like we'd done in Hawaii, we faked – dramatized – the entrance of each contestant on the show. This time we had eight individuals, four men and four women, no couples. On the first morning I was positioned on the dirt road to the ranch with the producer, ready to greet the contestants. The contestants had been isolated from each other, finally meeting on camera at the ranch.

Each contestant was driven to the ranch gate in a cab where we had a classic old pickup truck waiting to transport them onto the show on camera. I instructed them one by one to get their luggage out of the cab and toss it into the pickup's bed. One contestant stood out. She exited her cab with a flourish. She was dressed more for a night at the disco than for a day on the ranch. She had big hair, blonde and piled high, and was wearing a halter top, hot pants and high heels. She asked me who would get her luggage for her and who could get her a cup of coffee. Oh boy, we've got a live one. I told her that no one was here to wait on her, to move her luggage into the truck herself, and to get a move on. She strutted like a model, not the best approach for herding cattle. Let's call her Barbie.

Once the final contestant arrived we set up to start the show in earnest. Rocco greeted them, standing by a line of hay bales with their luggage piled on top. He welcomed them and told them that their life, as they knew it, was left behind. They were on a ranch now and had to follow the rules to get along. He told them that the show would outfit them with everything they needed, from clothes to toiletries, and that their luggage and belongings would be kept safe and returned to them when they left. He then instructed each one to open their luggage and keep one thing – just one thing.

Barbie opened her suitcase on camera. She pondered for a moment and finally chose a hairbrush, telling Rocco that she had a thousand-dollar hair weave and needed the brush to maintain it. Rocco's a big guy – tough as any cowboy and sweet as fresh strawberries. He smiled as she accepted her situation.

* * *

Barbie continued to be a handful. On her first day she complained about everything but we pushed her along with the others. That was too much for her, and on the second day she demanded to leave the show. The producer reminded her that she had signed a contract and that the planned challenges were designed for eight contestants. She didn't care and demanded to speak to her lawyer. After much hand-wringing the producer relented and escorted her to a phone.

There aren't many phones on a working ranch beyond the ranch house, but there was a phone jack in one of the outbuildings and a phone was plugged in for her. We left her alone to talk to her lawyer. Since we had already started the shoot day, she had a wireless mic on and nobody thought to turn it off. I don't remember how, but a PA heard her end of the call and reported to me after she was done.

She claimed all sorts of abuse when in fact she was simply describing the hard work required on any ranch. But her main complaint was that she claimed to have been told by the casting agent that she would be the 'Paris Hilton' of the show and could ride her exposure into an acting career. Baloney ! We sent her home before the end of the first week. That's reality.

APD Recruitment

The Albuquerque Police Department was in the same pickle as most other cities' safety departments, regaining officers to fill its ranks. Fifteen years ago the department called for filmmakers to create recruitment videos to entice candidates to join. A panel, including the chief of police and various public safety officials, screened a handful of prospective directors, me included. I got the job by yucking it up with the panel, telling them the crazy story of the Dept. of Transportation chief and his insistence on a somewhat pornographic slogan to end a breathalyzer ad : "Don't drink and drive or you may end up blowing more than your date." I had the room in the palm of my hands. Remember what I said about manipulation ?

Based on specs for the job enumerated by the Chief of Police and the PIO (public information officer), I got busy writing a series of ads with a proposed budget nearing $250,000. To my dismay, the Department PIO informed me that they only had $50,000 to spend. They had Champagne taste with a beer budget. Merde !

Always resourceful, I countered that I could meet their budget if they granted me full access to Police Department officers and resources. They agreed.

At the time, it cost upwards of $10,000 an hour plus fuel and insurance to hire a helicopter, they let me use theirs. Hiring actors and dressing them as a SWAT team would be expensive, the real SWAT team showed up with an assault tank to film in my neighborhood. Even officers on horseback and underwater divers were made available. It made for a successful ad campaign that was a hoot to produce.

The SWAT team charged into a house to rescue a kidnapped mother and child. The shot of a SWAT officer rushing out of the house with a toddler in only a diaper was dynamic. We shot them breaking through the door and using a flash-bang grenade, but the mayor objected to using the shot in the campaign.

Why would the department have divers and a hovercraft in the New Mexico desert ? Because there are rivers and lakes in the surrounding counties. There's a lovely park with three small lakes near downtown Albuquerque called Tingley Beach that had been renovated recently and drew lots of locals for fishing. The largest of the three lakes wasn't very wide or deep but my DP, John Britt, made it look like the Great Lakes with clever camera angles. Officers with automatic weapons zipped by on their hovercraft, and divers recovered a discarded weapon from the bottom of the lake.

I envisioned a low-angle shot on the water to see a diver break the surface with a gun he'd retrieved, but the officers informed me that it would be fake. In real life, they'd take a plastic tub to the bottom and scoop up all of the muck surrounding the gun to preserve any additional evidence. We took their advice and adjusted our shot. Not as sexy, but authentic.

The bar scene on Central Avenue downtown on Saturday night was a trip. Each weekend night the city would close Central Avenue from 1st to 8th streets to protect the crowds of bar-hopping revelers. Lots of uniformed officers mingled in the crowds.

Starting around 10PM there were four mounted officers positioned at the corner of 4th Street, ready to intervene. Each bar had a bouncer at the door with a flashlight. Rather than shout for help they'd simply shine their flashlight on the head of a troublemaker who would quickly be confronted by an officer on a huge horse. Very intimidating.

My son, Miles, got into the act, playing a drunk shouting and stumbling down the street. To subdue him, the mounted officers would flank him, reach down to grab his hands, then twist his wrists causing him to rise up on his toes to walk with no chance of resisting. The shot looked great but the mayor wouldn't let us use that one, either. It looked too intimidating.

I cast Keaton with a friend as juveniles running from patrol cars. We secured permission from Walgreens to shoot in their parking lot. The scene had Keaton and his buddy run behind the store as two squad cars screeched to a stop and officers bounded out of their cars to catch them.

Keaton was caught by an officer as he attempted to scale a wall. The officer then pressed him against his car as he cuffed him. But Keaton was a fighter with martial arts training, a tall, skinny teen with a chip on his shoulder. He wanted to have some fun, so he asked the officer to get a little rough, slamming him onto the squad car's trunk to control him. We shot seven takes. His upper arm and shoulder were bruised and he loved every minute of it. The scene was shot from the helicopter circling over the store.

The effort was a success. I delivered three 30-second spots for airing on local channels and a 2-minute video for use by recruiters visiting other states. My only mistake was to exclude the Chief of Police from a part in any of the spots. The Chief was a great guy and very effective, but he was tiny, not the buff example of a lawman that I'd hoped to portray. I should have found a way to include him in the ad campaign – my mistake.

I love working with cops.

 The APD commercials can be viewed on my site on YouTube at : https://www.youtube.com/watch?v=hbFJ6Vkn9Ew

The Golden Headset Award

I've had a lot of luck in my career in entertainment. For over 40 years I worked in film and TV, produced and voiced tons of radio and TV commercials, produced and directed stage plays, was a lead actor in musicals, and taught filmmaking to hungry college students. Most of those opportunities came to me. Reputation is everything.

Case in point: I got a call from a publisher in Albuquerque asking if I'd like to narrate an audiobook. I have a pretty clear voice, but up to that point all of my voice recordings were for 30-second commercials. I jumped at the chance.

The book was a Western and, back in those days, the publisher contracted for studio recording time with an audio engineer responsible for the recording. All I had to do was read. The process has changed over the years. Most audio work is now done at the narrator's home and sent to the producer digitally.

The publisher was happy with my first book and invited me to do another, then another. That filled my next five years in between film gigs. In total I voiced seventy titles, much of it pulp fiction, cowboy tales, and action stories.

My favorites were three mysteries penned by Max Allen Collins whose novel *The Road to Perdition* was made into a feature film starring Tom Hanks. Max wrote a series of murder mysteries that took place during otherwise historic events, his disaster series. I voiced *The Titanic Murders,* *The Pearl Harbor Murders,* and *The Hindenburg Murders.*

I was dismissive when the publisher told me that I'd been nominated for an award for two of my narrations. What's the big deal ? Then the awards were announced. I had won the Golden Headset Award for *The Hindenburg Murders.* That made me sit up and take notice.

The Golden Headset Awards were announced annually by critic Bennet Pomerantz in his *Audioworld* magazine column in a range of categories covering varied audio productions. There were ten categories. I was nominated in the inspirational category but lost to James Earl Jones reading *The Bible,* like I had a chance ! But I won in the unabridged fiction category for *The Hindenburg Murders.* It was a complicated production for which I voiced the crew and passengers on the airship, including male and female Americans, Italians and French characters.

Of the ten winners that year I was the only unknown talent. There were four established audiobook veterans plus James Earl Jones, Phyllis Diller, Annette Benning, and Tim Curry. I had won in my category over fellow nominees Burt Reynolds and Artie Johnson. WOW ! I'll take that company any day !

* * *

There wasn't any ceremony to grant the awards. There wasn't even a physical award. So my good friend, Tom, bought a cheap headset at Radio Shack, cut off the cable, sprayed it gold, and threw a party. My fabulous neighbors presented me with the trophy and we all got toasted !

The PIT

The basketball arena at The University of New Mexico is world famous. It's called The PIT because the playing floor is thirty-eight feet below ground. In the year 2000, *Sports Illustrated* ran an article listing the 20 best sports venues of the century worldwide, all sports included. The PIT was number 13. Why so famous ?

When it was built in the mid '60s the University had just a million bucks to dedicate to the project. So the architect concocted a unique plan to dig a huge hole with sloped sides and pour concrete directly on the dirt, eliminating the need to construct wooden forms to form the seating areas. Construction started by building the roof. Then they dug the hole, protected from weather above. The result was a relatively small arena, 15,000 seats, with seating areas on steep slopes, bringing the fans closer to the court. An added bonus was the noise level created by the design, a true sixth man when the crowd roared, an amazing home-court advantage. Some years later a mezzanine and 2,000 seats were added below the roof.

I was a professor in the Theater Department in 2010 when the University announced a sixty-million-dollar renovation of the PIT, $60,000,000. I'm a boy. I love trucks and construction, so I approached the Athletic Department, proposing to film the renovation. At first they balked, but as the planning progressed, it was mentioned that there were no films or photos of the original construction. My proposal was approved. They budgeted $60,000 dollars for my company to produce the 18-month project. That number doubled including the production of 10,000 DVDs to be given to season ticket holders at the grand re-opening and sold in the gift shop.

At first I hired a crew to shoot the project but realized quickly that the budget was too slim, so I shot for 15 months myself. We mounted a time-lapse camera on a university building across the street to capture the demo of the exterior and the rise of the new, metal superstructure. I hired musician friends to create a knockoff of the song "Spinning Wheel", you know, "What goes up, must come down…." It was a perfect theme for the demo of the building's exterior.

I added a hard hat and safety boots to my gear and relied on my partner, Randy McComas, to prep the camera for shooting. Randy would also direct the edit. The rough and tumble construction workers tolerated me but rolled their eyes, wondering what the hell I was doing there. Midway through construction, the athletic Dept. hosted a lunch to boost the morale of the workers. There were dozens of companies involved from Ironworkers and electricians to plumbers and glass installers. We had a lot of footage at that point and Randy cut together a 2-minute video featuring close-ups of the workers that we showed at the lunch. Backed by upbeat music, the video showed the men hard at it, almost heroic. They appreciated our gesture and treated me as one of the guys from then on.

We interviewed the original architect for the film and scoured the archives at the UNM library for any original construction plans. We were lucky to find a thousand black-and-white photos from the 1967 construction, buried in the basement archives. The archivist was just months from retiring, and she was the only one on the library staff who knew of the pictures. Saved by the bell!

Amazingly, the basketball teams played a full season during construction. Each game required a special use permit to allow fans into the building. There were over seventy special-use permits issued after fully completed inspections by engineers and fire officials, and the fans tolerated walking outside to visit concession stands in the parking lot under tents and rows of port-a-potties. As a professor and an Alum, I was a huge fan. For five years I'd served as floor director for all broadcast basketball games.

The men's team won the division that year and the women's team drew crowds exceeding 7,000 fans making for great additions to the video. I shot most games and, unlike news photogs, I had free rein to shoot from wherever I pleased. In the end I should have charged double, but I had a ball and don't regret a minute of it.

In Plain Sight

In Plain Sight was a cop show about witness protection starring Mary McCormack and Frederick Weller. Every episode started with a crime in an American city and the witnesses were assigned to protection in Albuquerque. Parts of Albuquerque and the surrounding area stood in for the distant cities in the episodes.

One episode was written with a crime at the waterfront in Boston. Although the Rio Grande River runs through the center of town it's pretty shallow and not at all suited to docks. Locally the river is nicknamed Rio Poquito, or Little River. Production faked the opening shot brilliantly, placing a camera between two large warehouse buildings and shooting towards the railroad tracks. FX laid down a thick fog over the tracks and the sound designer added the air horn of a passing tugboat. They faked the Boston docks on dry land at minimal cost. Very effective.

* * *

Most of my work on the show was as the EPK director, filming behind the scenes and interviewing the cast and crew, but on one episode I got a treat. The episode revolved around a high school basketball player who was betting on his games with a crooked bookie, and was deep in debt.

A game was staged in a high school gym with a packed crowd in the stands. The episode director was an observer that day as the producer hired a co-director with a background in shooting sports to shoot the action on the court. Then I was hired to get the crowds riled up for shots of them reacting to the game. The crowd reaction shots were accomplished while the basketball players took a break. The crowd was reacting to my overblown antics on the court. I had a ball. What a thrill to entice hundreds of extras to cheer by acting the fool for their enjoyment.

The show's star, Mary McCormack, watched my 'clown act' and commented to a friend on the crew that I must have a big heart. Awww, shucks.

America's Most Wanted

John Walsh – *America's Most Wanted*

Shooting in the desert with John Walsh on *America's Most Wanted*. John's on a Harley. I'm ducking behind cacti, ready to cue him. Celebrities carry an aura filled with the reality of who they are, from humble and grateful to arrogant and reclusive. John embodies the humble, grateful type.

The public loves John Walsh and Law Enforcement loves him even more. We needed a Harley for a shot in Albuquerque, so I contacted a local dealer who went the extra mile, delivering two classic Harleys for John to pick from, no charge.

Then there was the breakfast rush… filmmakers ALWAYS feed the crew.

We were prepping to join a wagon train of Law Enforcement vehicles serving warrants in neighborhoods. I contracted with a church in Albuquerque's South Valley to stage in their parking lot and to serve breakfast to the camera crew and all of the officers, about 25 officers and a small film crew.

But word got out amongst law enforcement that John Walsh would be there and another 80 Police Officers and Sheriff's Deputies showed up just to shake his hand and take a selfie.

There was no option but to extend the invitation for a fresh, hot breakfast to everyone present. The caterer agreed and rushed off for more eggs and bacon, leaving two cooks to keep the food truck serving.

The result was a Law Enforcement shindig with 100 officers from varied agencies all eating together in a Church fellowship hall. Yeehaaaaah !

Serving Warrants with
America's Most Wanted

A show like *America's Most Wanted* will use any location to shoot intros to stories they're covering. And law enforcement agencies suggested actions that we could cover.

So we tagged along on a mission to serve arrest warrants in various locations around Albuquerque. At each location we'd film Mr. Walsh on camera, setting up the arrest and perp walk behind him.

Albuquerque police were in the lead. I watched the caravan take shape. Police motorcycles in the lead, followed by various SUV's and sedans, all unmarked, displaying their lights but maintaining siren silence. Mr. Walsh was in one of the lead cars.

There was a windowless van with its seats replaced by two benches along the side walls. Eight SWAT officers in full gear and face masks looked ominous as the back doors were closed.

Wait a second. We need to get a production van in this caravan for the camera crew. The lead officer designated a place for us in the line and we took off.

My son, Keaton, was a PA that day. He was there to help. Keaton had talked of working in some law enforcement capacity since he was little. So I asked him to drive the van. YeeeeHaaaa ! Eighteen years old and speeding through 8-lane intersections like a scene from *Lethal Weapon*.

The eight-vehicle caravan raced through major intersections with motorcycle units blocking traffic. Keaton kept the pace.

Our first stop was an eye opener. We raced into a neighborhood with vehicles stopping every which way like you see on TV. The difference was that every officer pulled a weapon and surveyed every window in the area.

Picture that. A dozen armed officers training their sights on every house and window in the vicinity. This was reality, not reality TV.

Keaton told me later that he'd learned that they train weapons at every house in case a criminal associate in a neighboring house tries to shoot at them while they serve the warrant at the target house. Nobody wants to get shot in the back.

There's a scene in the first episode of *Breaking Bad* where Aaron Paul escapes pantsless out an upstairs window while law enforcement barges in the front door. It wouldn't happen in real life but it made for good TV !

Who's Playing Lead Guitar ?

After working with *America's Most Wanted* in New Mexico I was invited to join them for a shoot at the Charlotte Motor Speedway in North Carolina.

We set a camera position for John to do intros with the cars racing past, just behind him on the track. Intros are the short scripts where an anchor teases the next story and then 'throws' to the reporter on the scene.

I was the AD so I'd cue John when the race cars would be behind him. It was a thrill. Who gets to stand in the infield 30 feet from the track at the Charlotte Motor Speedway as cars roared by. This is a GREAT career.

After the intros we set up for a promo spot with John positioned in front of a semi with a large logo displayed on its side, parked in the infield. We positioned John in front of the truck and got camera and sound ready. Suddenly a rock band started wailing 80 yards away. Shit ! We couldn't record clean sound with all that racket.

I called cut and took off running to silence the band. They were rehearsing for a show later that night. The producer sent a PA in a golf cart to drive me to the stage but they never caught me. I was cookin'. I ran the 100-yard dash in college, but that was 20 years in the past.

I got to the stage and somehow got the attention of the lead guitarist. His back was to me and he was wailing away on his guitar.

Then he turned. It was Kevin Costner, no shit ! Who knew he had a band !? He was very kind. I told him the situation and asked if he could hold off for ten minutes while we got our shot. He smiled and offered a quid pro quo: he'd chill if I'd introduce him to John Walsh. Deal ! John spent some time with Kevin in his trailer when we were done.

At wrap, the producer treated the crew to a splendid dinner. We partied into the wee hours on his credit card.

A Personal Journey

Forks In The Road

Many of us squander away years, working jobs rather than focusing on a career, living care free and partying away our potential. My journey included stints as a car painter, line cook, bottled water delivery driver, video tape operator, childcare worker, still photographer and pot dealer. I was in my late 20s when I got the urge to focus on a career.

That's when I got the bug to become a film director from Charlie Chaplin. In his classic films, *City Lights, The Great Dictator,* and *Modern Times* Charlie offers life lessons carefully woven into comic routines, a subtle approach to bettering our society without preaching.

So I enrolled in college.

UNM Theatre

Hoping to become a filmmaker, I enrolled in cinema classes at UNM, the University of New Mexico. In the first year I realized that the film teacher was literally insane and the TV production teacher was a drunk. Not much to learn here, I was outta there.

On the way out the door I was grabbed by a professor who invited me to join the theater program. That changed my life. All I wanted was to learn to direct films, but there were other plans afoot.

I got a work/study job assisting the top professor in the department, Dr. Bob Hurtung*, Daddy Bob to us all. Bob had retired from a long career starting on Broadway and continuing to early network TV, writing teleplay adaptations for *The Hallmark Hall Of Fame*. He co-produced the productions and was consistently nominated for awards from the WGA, *Writers Guild of America*.

He was happy to direct college plays and mentor young writing and acting talent. Bob decided that I'd be in his talent pool. The first audition was for a musical, *The Travelin' Show*. It was a singing audition.

In my first year of college, at the University of Scranton, I had joined the choir but I was in it more for the beer than for the music. I had some raw talent but no style or discipline. Now I had to belt a song for Bob and a former Broadway conductor that Bob had enticed to join the UNM Music Dept.

I gave it my all. The part I was auditioning for was a dancing, singing Chinese villain, and I wanted it. When my song was done, Bob and the music director met me side stage. They didn't mince words. They were in agreement that: A, it was a terrible audition and B, I got the part. They saw my potential. It was my first chance to be on stage.

With Miles backstage in Rodey Theatre at UNM. As theatre students, we performed on the Rodey stage 30 years apart. Photo by Dan Peebles

My work as Daddy Bob's assistant, coupled with acting in his productions, made the college experience a thrill. We staged a musical by Christopher Durang: *The History of American Film.* It's a comedy that bombed in New York but was a big hit in LA. I was cast to play two roles: Charleton Heston, imploring the audience to enjoy the offerings on the silver screen, and Al Jolson, singing a medley of "Swanee River" and "Mammy" in blackface. It was the late seventies and any pictures of the production are long gone. Lucky me.

A few years with Bob at UNM and I was ready to tackle the world. And my dream had expanded. I not only wanted to direct films, now I wanted to act, too. And what about music. A month into joining the choir at The University of Scranton I'd been named the baritone soloist.

Hmmmmmm; acting, singing, directing…. My dream expanded to the hope of being nominated for an Oscar, a Tony, an Emmy and a Grammy. It can be done. Whoopi Goldberg did it. So did Rita Moreno and Mel Brooks. I was pumped ! I had a dream.

ACLOA

In the summer of '82 I was hired by local director, Fred Maio, to help stage *The Sound of Music.* The initial assignment was to direct the child actors in the Von Trapp family, but expanded to co-directing the production. The play was produced by ACLOA, the Albuquerque

Civic Light Opera Association, the largest community theater company in the country at the time. We played in Popejoy Hall, a 2,000-seat theater, and we put 1,500 butts in seats on average nights. It was pretty big for a community theater.

ACLOA's '82 summer schedule included *The Sound of Music* and *Stop The World – I Want To Get Off.* Fred had been hired to direct both. During our rehearsals on The Sound of Music I was asked by a theater friend if I was auditioning for *Stop The World* but I hadn't thought of it. I'd never heard of the play or the music. That night he turned me on to the Broadway soundtrack. I was transported. Each song was better than the last, and the lead vocals were perfect for my range. The story told in the songs was clear yet I hadn't read the 'book' yet. In musicals, the play minus the songs is referred to as 'the book.'

I got a copy of the play, prepared an audition, and got the lead, Littlechap, the only adult male in the cast.

Littlechap is a randy fellow, chatting up all the birds on the block, (it's British), until he knocks up the boss's daughter. British actor Anthony Newley wrote the play for himself; a troupe of circus clowns in a big top with no set or costume changes and no props. It's all pantomime. Not easy.

The cast includes Littlechap, his wife Evie, his two daughters, and seven female clowns. For a leading man, it's like dancing in a bed of roses ! There were a few hits from the show: "Gonna Build A Mountain", and the showstopper "What Kind of Fool Am I", made famous in the US by Sammy Davis, Jr.

Newley and his partner, Leslie Bricusse, also wrote the music for *Willie Wonka and The Chocolate Factory* including "The Candy Man" and "Pure Imagination", also made famous by Mr. Davis.

One of my daughters was played by a young Heidi Swedberg who went on to play George's unlucky fiancé on *Seinfeld* among other TV and movie roles. My wife was played by Carolyn Ward, newly pregnant and strutting the stage bravely in tights. The only male in the script, besides Littlechap, was a 5-year-old boy who pantomimes being born a few times in the play. He has no lines. The part was played by Anthony Strascina who went on to make his mark in Christian rock under the name Tony Vincent.

I got great reviews from the Albuquerque papers and local TV reviewers, a solid hit. Fifteen thousand people saw the play over twelve shows, showering us with standing ovations every night. It's a thrill to stand on stage while fifteen hundred people stand and cheer for you.

After each show we were swamped in the Green Room by members of the audience, still applauding our performance. The biggest thrill for me was a pat on the back from the son of Emmett Kelly, a world-renowned clown.

My hope going forward was that I'd find my way out of the Southwest and onto the Broadway stage. I asked my mentor, Daddy Bob, to come see the play. After closing, I visited with Bob. He'd seen the play twice and was very supportive. He told me that I had plenty of talent for Broadway, I just had to get there and take my chances.

I have a strong baritone voice so I knew I'd have a shot at the chorus of any show even if I didn't get a part. I was flying high. Three years previous I was hoping to become a Hollywood film director, now I had my sights on Broadway.

Then it happened. On my way home from work at the Children's Psychiatric Center, late at night, I crashed my bike without a helmet. I slid down the road, riding the asphalt on my face. I was a bloody mess. I picked up the bike and headed back to the hospital. The nurse who'd just sent me home couldn't recognize my damaged, blood-soaked face.

Doctors at UNM hospital sewed me up and sent me home. Forty stitches closed a gash in my forehead at the hairline above my right eye, but there was no follow-up.

It was 1983. No one would be talking about Traumatic Brain Injuries, TBI, for another twenty years when the NFL started banging the drum. It wasn't until nearly 40 years later, in 2020, that neurologists helped me understand the lingering effects of the brain damage from the bike accident.

Looking back on it now, I realize the extent of the personality change brought on by the TBI. Overnight I'd lost the ability to perform in public. It's central to any performing art to declare 'look at me,' as an actor, singer, poet. I went from lead actor, singing to 1,500 people a night, to house manager, unable to sing out loud if anyone was listening. I'd lost my edge, my courage.

Dreams Denied

So, what is a TBI ? How the hell should I know. There are plenty of websites explaining the physical damage that results from a concussion or TBI, but what are the continuing effects ? Apparently it's different for each victim depending on the severity of the brain injury, the part of the brain that's affected, and the mental health condition of the victim prior to the injury.

But across the board, survivors report that they know that they've changed and don't understand it. Doctor Michael Pendleton, a brilliant Chiropractic Neurologist who treated me, summed it up in a video on his website. He said that TBI victims often face friends and relatives who discount their struggles. They'll say, "You're OK, you're just depressed." Of course they're depressed, they know that something's wrong and have no idea how to deal with it.

I recently read an interview with George Clooney. He reported that he'd suffered a TBI on the film *Syriana*. He shared that the injury led to thoughts of suicide because he "couldn't go on living like that."

Living like what ? That's my question. As far as I can see the 'what' will be different for each survivor. For Clooney there were follow-up surgeries due to actual fluid leakage from his brain. He's better now, acting and directing, and married to the most intelligent woman in the world, Human Rights Lawyer Amal Alamuddin. Maybe there's a chance for me yet !?

* * *

I suffered my TBI in '83 – a terrible bicycle crash with no helmet. I split my head open requiring forty stitches at the hairline above my right eye plus more stitches on the right side of my face. I couldn't walk in a straight line for years, always running into doorjambs when I tried to simply walk through a door. I'd lost all sense of balance. I had to give up tennis and basketball.

The docs sewed up my head and sent me home. I don't remember much from the time, but one thing for sure is that there was zero medical follow-up. I had no idea that I'd need further help and guidance. It's only in the past few years that I realized the immense personality shift caused by the injury forty years previous.

Part of the confusion was a drastic change in living circumstances. For the 5 years prior to the accident, I'd focused on a career in theater. Co-directing *The Sound of Music* and playing the lead in *Stop The World* that summer was a giant step towards a desired career on Broadway. But my life had changed.

I had invited a female friend, Johanna Johnson, to see the show, hoping to sweep her off her feet. She had performed in *Stop The World* in high school, it was an easy hook. She showed up one Saturday and changed my world.

I was thunderstruck. Suddenly true love trumped career goals.

The accident happened only weeks into my relationship with Johanna and, with no prodding from docs to seek medical care, I marched on with zero acknowledgment or understanding of the lingering effects.

* * *

For the better part of 35 years suicidal ideation was an almost daily occurrence. That stopped once the TBI was diagnosed in 2020. Years before I had made a pact with myself that suicide was never an option. The problem, as I saw it, was that suicide just transfers your pain to the loved ones who miss you. Besides, I didn't want to die. I just wanted the fog to lift.

It's now four years later and I'm in recovery. Treatments by two Chiropractic Neurologists at the Southwest Brain Performance Center sparked my recovery with months of biofeedback and bodywork. Thank you Dr. Michael Pendleton and Dr. Doug Meintz.

In Virginia Beach I received EMDR therapy. The result is a vast improvement in my short-term memory and, most importantly, a resurgence of confidence and courage. Life is still a challenge but it's a lot better now that I understand the hurdles.

There are two plans going forward : finding a therapist in the military with experience with TBI, and medical treatment at the Hino Clinic in Ensenada, Mexico. That's where the NFL sends players suffering from repeated concussions. I've been accepted as a patient but need to raise the cash for the treatment and the travel, about $18,000 bucks. Health insurance doesn't cover anything regarding TBI. It's expensive and all out of pocket.

* * *

What happens to a dream deferred ?
Does it dry up
Like a raisin in the sun ?
Or fester like a sore –
And then run ?
Does it stink like rotten meat ?
Or crust and sugar over –
Like a syrupy sweet ?

Maybe it just sags
Like a heavy load

or does it explode ?

Langston Hughes

Looking Back

Since the diagnosis I've looked back at the past 40 years, hoping to untangle the confusion that had imprisoned me.

Some of the effects of the injury were obvious: severe lack of balance, total loss of senses of smell and taste, memory issues, and depression.

Prior to the injury I enjoyed an "A" personality, displaying courage and confidence. That was gone, replaced by a desire to remain in the background, isolated.

Especially frustrating was a habit of starting personal projects that cost money and time and never panned out. I mistakenly thought that the therapies in 2020 and '21 had restored me to the young, courageous entertainer that I was prior to the injury.

Most of all I wanted to get back to performing.

I moved to Virginia Beach to join my son and grandson. I bought a wireless speaker system with mics and stands to revive my love of singing, hoping to join musicians and offer concerts in the parks. It was five thousand bucks down the drain. I spent more time and money creating videos and planning a presence on social media when I knew that I was incapable of handling the day-to-day chores of staying in touch with subscribers. Technology hasn't been a friend. And I continue to struggle with personal contacts.

Prior to the injury I was always surging ahead, always a success. I now struggle with 'social anxiety disorder.' Broadly, that speaks of an awkwardness in public, but it's more pronounced than that. I'm continually frustrated by memory issues, causing me to avoid and isolate. It's especially problematic at gatherings, like church.

Every week at church I'm approached by friends that I know, that I've had extended conversations with, but I can't remember who they are and why I know them. It's not Alzheimer's; it's a residual effect from the TBI, but it makes me feel dumb and disconnected. Who wouldn't run from that ? Isolation is at least something that I understand.

The same was true on film sets, especially *Breaking Bad* and *Better Call Saul* because I was with that crew for five years. I was able to establish connections with some of the crew but the rest were a blur. Friends noted my 'cute habit' of calling men 'bubba' and women 'darling,' not realizing that it was a cover because I couldn't recall their names. At home, I call my son and grandson by nicknames because I often can't remember their names quickly enough. The neurologists explained my memory issues, likening my brain to a filing cabinet. All of the information was retained but often wasn't accessible, like locked drawers. Sounds like no big deal, but it made socializing a minefield. Many people take it personally when you can't recall their names, or, even worse, when you have no recollection of who they are or having met them.

Social anxiety and loneliness walk hand in hand – after a difficult divorce in the mid '90s I was only graced with two short-lived romances – one for 2 years and another for three. I spent 20 of the last 25 years lonely and depressed. I'm a family man at heart, never meant for the single life, so the loneliness accelerated my need to medicate with alcohol and pot – bushels of pot. I was lucky to have pot as my drug of choice. Any heavier med would have drowned me.

My good friend, Ann Lerner, recently remarked that I hid my challenges well. Ann has been a close friend and work associate for 35 years and never noticed my internal hell. When I shared these pages with her, she was astounded by the depth of my struggle, remarking through her tears that I hid it well – an unfortunate accomplishment.

The greatest challenge has been an inability to sequence, as noted in my original diagnosis. The world now runs on computer programs and they all function on a series of prompts – sequences. Personal computers didn't hit the scene until the '90s. Prior to that, applying for work and contact with doctors were done on paper or on the phone.

I started in the film industry in 1987. I walked into a production office and handed my resume to a production coordinator. By the mid '90s, after working on *Young Guns II* and *City Slickers,* my reputation preceded me, and I no longer needed to look for work. Work looked for me. That continued into teaching at The University of New Mexico and Central NM Community College – they called me, offering faculty positions.

Now, in retirement, I'm faced with a computer-driven world that is nearly impossible for me to navigate. Contact with doctors is all online. Seeking most employment is done online. In the film world and as a college professor, there were always assistants to help with technology, not so in retirement.

I'd hoped to return to narrating audiobooks but finding books to be narrated and auditioning is all online now. Plus most sites expect you to be the narrator and your own engineer. Twenty years ago I narrated 70 titles for one publisher spanning five years in a studio with a professional engineer. The world has moved past me and I'm struggling to catch up.

* * *

I mentioned that the injury took away my sense of taste and smell permanently but there was more. Loss of short-term memory made simple tasks harder. Countless times I walked into a room and stood motionless, wondering why I was there. I'd trace my steps and often see a clue that sparked my memory and I'd get what I came for. Sounds like no big deal but when it's your everyday default it gets annoying.

At CNM, Central NM Community College, the film program was housed miles away from the main campus so we seldom saw any administrators. One day the Dean introduced me to the VP of the college who was touring our building. We shook hands and exchanged pleasantries.

About a year later I ran into him on campus. He greeted me by name, cheerily, but was annoyed when I asked who he was. Jump ahead another year and it happens again. But this time it wasn't enough for him to be annoyed, now I needed to be punished. He shut down a program that I'd prepared with another instructor for the good of the college : to teach life-saving CPR to all students, teachers, and staff.

I had made a lasting friendship with the head instructor in the EMT program and we collaborated on making videos to teach hands-only CPR. It was a class project that took months of preparation, production, and post-production resulting in a great learning experience for the students and a great video for the EMT program. Knowing the importance of CPR training and, with video in hand, I approached the administration, suggesting that the CPR classes and the training video be made available to all students, teachers and staff. It was all positive and we were certain that the project would be approved. But the vindictive VP shut it down, a loss for the community based on a misunderstanding.

Another behavior that troubled me was a habit of crying for no apparent reason. At first it seemed that the tendency to choke up was connected to inspired performances like Dorothy singing "Somewhere Over The Rainbow" in *The Wizard of Oz* but that was short-sighted.

The neurologists opined that the area of my brain damaged in the accident governed my reaction to passion and thus led to emotional responses. Hmmmmm ?

Like most of us, I chose to stuff it rather than explore the discomfort. There are times when it hits me outta the blue and I stuff it fast, in about 5 seconds. That's all I'll allow myself to feel whatever it is. I found relief in going on long drives and singing showstopper Broadway hits with tears streaming down my cheeks.

I suspect a couple of initiators for the choking up : A) when I watch a video of an actor excelling on a song I tighten up because I want to be there. I know that I can do that but I'm blocked by the injury or B) I have no idea what's wrong and need help finding the answer.

* * *

With all of that, I still feel blessed. I never reached my potential but I was still able to thrive in two rewarding careers : as a filmmaker and as a college instructor. Writing this book is a step towards continued engagement with the world. It's fulfilling my need to create while protecting my solitude.

Up, Up and Away

Sky Warriors – The Road To Recovery

Sky Warriors was a program at CNM supporting Military Veterans challenged by PTSD and TBI. The program enlisted Military Veterans to serve on a team, launching and chasing hot air balloons. It was a way to help Vets socialize. There's an ongoing epidemic of suicides among veterans, about 22 vets kill themselves each day, so outreach to Veterans is a must.

It was an interview during Sky Warriors that started my quest for answers, my road to recovery. I had heard of TBI related to retired NFL players. Online articles exposed the confusion and isolation experienced by players as a result of multiple concussions. The same was true for Military Veterans, although their injuries are more likely from a single battlefield incident.

The program was initiated by the Dean of Students, Dr. Rudy Garcia, in cooperation with the Veteran's

Resource Center on campus. Rudy was an avid balloonist. He recruited Diana and Randy Mykelbust and their balloon to create the experience.

Vets respond to group tasks. During their careers in the military, they worked as teams, with constant personal interactions. All of that goes away once the Vet enters civilian life, a world of individuals and isolation.

So Rudy, Diana and Randy gathered a handful of Vets and proceeded to train them as a team, to assemble and fly a hot air balloon. It was an exhilarating experience for all of us, including the student film crew.

I met Rudy at his office, needing guidance regarding a student. When I told him that I taught filmmaking he immediately started to pitch the Sky Warriors program. He asked if we'd be interested in filming the project. I jumped at the chance.

One of the greatest perks in the film industry is the randomness of it all, and I enjoyed exposing my students to it. Most people go to work at the same time and place every day. Not so for filmmakers. For the Sky Warriors project, the students had a 5 AM call time in a Dunkin' Donuts parking lot, and then a quick caravan to a deserted field to assemble and launch the balloon.

To personalize the action shots, we peppered the video with short interviews with the Vets. That's when I got the clue that I had a problem. It was during an interview with an Army Vet struggling with the effects of a TBI suffered in combat.

He spoke of his need to isolate. When I asked how he navigated the college environment he said that the teamwork with the Sky Warriors had helped him : "I was pretty confined, prior to Sky Warriors. I'd come here and register and leave as quick as I could. If somebody blinked an eye I'd vanish, you know." He went on to say that working with the Sky Warriors and the Veteran's Resource group had helped him come out of his shell.

That story stuck with me. I realized that I had similar tendencies. I spent my workdays surrounded by busy professionals on film sets and was effective in my work relationships. But once the workday was done, I was off to my cave. Leave me alone. And I'd done it for decades, drawing others to me and then pushing them away to be alone again, with the sadness and confusion that resulted.

It was that realization that led me to the Neurologists at Southwest Brain Performance Center.

Side note : Whenever possible I'd take students onto film sets to get them excited about starting a film career, or invite a star or producer to address the class. On Sky Warriors they got to meet and film Jonathan Banks from *Breaking Bad* and *Better Call Saul*. Jonathan opens the video with a statement praising the dedication of the Sky Warriors.

 You can see the video my YouTube channel, *Chuckie Did It,* at : https://www.youtube.com/watch?v=HrCzBc_dhQI&t=24s

How Could It Happen Twice ?

I was sitting in the Santa Fe office for the '91 TV movie *Into the Badlands* with Bruce Dern, Mariel Hemingway, Helen Hunt and Dermot Mulroney.

A robust film industry was still 25 years away for New Mexico so there were no designated film offices to rent. We made do at the Holiday Inn, booking a half dozen hotel rooms as offices on the first floor and rooms for talent and visiting crew upstairs.

The Holiday Inn was on the outskirts of town near the National Cemetery so there weren't any random individuals roaming around. I got a start when a tall, thin man with a scraggly beard and a rumpled baseball cap sauntered into our office. I didn't expect to encounter any vagrants out here on the edge of town. Lucky for me, I paused a moment and realized that it was our star, Bruce Dern, not a random straggler at all. He had just hit the hotel and was looking for his per diem. First encounters with movie stars… yikes !

Lesson learned − I thought.

A few years later, still in Santa Fe, I was production coordinator on *Gunsmoke: The Long Ride*. It was the fifth and last TV movie after the series ended. In the story, there's trouble for Marshall Dillon's daughter. We were filming at the Garson Studios situated on the campus of The College of Santa Fe.

During prep, a woman came in the office and, again, I mistook one of our stars for a lost soul. It was Ali McGraw, perfectly relaxed and sporting an 'I live here' Santa Fe look while running errands in town. She was playing the Marshall's daughter. Again, I caught myself before creating a faux pas.

We rely so heavily on the magical scrubbed persona of our stars as presented in movies and magazines. It's a shock to see them in real life.

Thanks for nuthin' *People* magazine !

Who's My Favorite Star ?

Sipping coffee with my friend Alex at Starbucks, solving the problems of the world. The conversation took a turn when she asked me about my experiences in the film biz. I can't resist anyone who's willing to listen to tales from the set.

Most people only see these stars on screen or in *People* magazine so details of behind-the-scenes shenanigans are swallowed up like a delicious dish of ice cream, with multiple flavors !

She asked me who was my favorite star, the one that I enjoyed working with the most. I quickly landed on Sam Jackson. I worked with Sam on *White Sands,* an espionage

thriller with a huge cast that was panned by *Rolling Stone.*
More on Sam and *White Sands* elsewhere in this book.

The film industry is a magical land, filled with brilliant,
creative people working tirelessly to craft stories for us all.
And the creativity and passion for the work stretches way
past the stars, writers and directors.

Everyone on the crew, from wardrobe and special
effects to the dolly grip, are dedicated to the team effort,
a mix of art and industry, SHOW BUSINESS. Watching
the Special Effects department work with local firemen to
construct rain towers for a windy, nasty night scene, is a
study in teamwork.

But back to my favorite star – I can't restrict it to one
person. It has to be a list : Sam Jackson, Jonathan Banks,
Bryan Cranston, Adam Sandler, Billy Crystal, Anna
Gunn, Mary Elizabeth Mastrantonio, Willem Dafoe, Bob
Odenkirk, Chloris Leachman, MoNique, James Arness,
John Forsyth, Victoria Principal … (help me, I can't stop)
… Randy Savage the Macho Man, Aaron Paul, Randy
Travis, Ruth Buzzi, Frank Zappa……..

Open Heart Surgery

1972 – I scored a job as a janitor at Harper Hospital
in Detroit. Harper was huge and was under renovation.
A new O.R. was being built with twenty-two operating
rooms, including two open heart rooms and two rooms for
Neurosurgery.

I was moved to the new O.R. when it opened, running a system of robot carts that carried supplies from floor to floor, delivering linens, patient meals and whatever. Similar carts were being used to collect and deliver mail in the Sears tower, stopping at each desk and ringing a little bell. I presume that the idea fizzled as I haven't heard about it since.

At Harper, the carts followed a wireless tracking system, traveling in tunnels under the hospital to designated elevators. I was very efficient in the new post and had lots of spare time to poke around.

Every operating room had a sliver of glass in their doors for communication with nurses. I spent countless hours watching whatever I could see as doctors and nurses huddled around each patient. After a time I was invited to scrub and witness surgeries up close. Open heart and neuro were the most interesting.

I was an excitable 23-year-old and the nurses and staff took to me. They recommended that I turn my interest into a career and train as a med tech. They were very supportive. In an effort to convince me to stay, the staff invited me to scrub and pass instruments on smaller cases like laryngoscopies. It was all fascinating but not for me. I was passing through.

The nurses were from around the globe and settled in Detroit from Puerto Rico, the Orient and every town USA. On Fridays we all brought our favorite dishes from home and enjoyed a sumptuous potluck lunch. I had some free time and a background as a line cook so it fell on me to set up the lunch. One Friday I was in the surgical prep area when a nurse stepped up to sterilize some surgical instruments. I had to ask her to wait a moment. I was reheating fried chicken in the autoclave.

Trauma – tainment

So much of TV relies on human frailty, personal shortcomings, natural tragedies and our increasingly toxic world.

I was a "stringer" for years, covering national stories happening locally, for the big three networks, ABC, NBC, and CBS. Those stories were always human tragedies resulting from crime and natural disasters, trauma-tainment. After awhile the cache of working big stories wears off as, once again, you shove a mic in a weary dad's face to ask him how hard it will be to rebuild while his family stands in the street staring at what's left of their home after a tornado.

Covering the Cerro Grande fire in Los Alamos, New Mexico, was eerie. The fire was in the pine covered mountains above the town but local law enforcement had called for a total evacuation, for good reason. The fire roared down canyons, consuming the homes and belongings of countless families in a fuel hungry rampage. 235 homes were lost.

Even with all of that chaos, the press was granted entrance to the town. We drove the empty streets looking for something to shoot for the story. Think of a scene from the film *Outbreak*, with streets empty of traffic except the occasional National Guard truck. Strip malls were vacant, no pedestrians, no joggers or dog walkers, a ghost town. There was occasional comic relief. One homeowner had taken his lawn sprinklers and set them on his roof. They oscillated, tick – tick – tick, repeatedly wetting the cedar shingled roof.

* * *

And dealing with young Network News assignment editors was a mixed blessing. Remember the "Runaway Bride" ? A white girl from a wealthy family got cold feet as her wedding approached, and ran away. When she surfaced, she claimed that she'd been kidnapped by black men in a van. The story unraveled and she had to admit making the whole thing up.

When she surrendered to authorities from a phone booth on Route 66 in central Albuquerque, I was sent with a camera crew to get the local angle for network news. She had been taken to a police substation to be questioned by the FBI. My crew set their shot with the substation in the background and we waited for the APD PIO (Albuquerque Police Dept – Public Information Officer) to come out and brief us.

We were set, ready. There another camera crew set up near us but the PIO knew me, and I was certain that she'd prioritize my camera for her first "stand-up."

That wasn't good enough for the assignment editor, squawking at me on the phone. I told her that the FBI was in the substation in a room with only high windows, no view or camera possibility. But that frustrated her. She wanted a shot NOW. She told me to bang on the window and get the FBI to hurry up and make a statement. Right ?!

When she was released, the Runaway Bride was escorted by police to catch a plane at the Albuquerque Sunport. A gaggle of press surrounded her as she walked to her plane, escorted by the APD PIO with a blanket over her head to hide her identity. My crew followed them to her right and the CNN crew shot from the left. Watching the news at home, my mom saw me in CNN's shot, shuffling along, mic in hand, covering the story.

* * *

Then there's the business side of trauma-tainment. I got a call to cover the manhunt for a killer in California. When the producer booked me I asked how long he expected me to be on the job. Since law enforcement was working with various leads he estimated that I'd be employed through the week, maybe longer. Those jobs pay well but they pay by the day with no job security. Imagine my disappointment when the killer was caught on the second day. Damn, a seriously mixed blessing, the public is safe but I'm broke.

* * *

The flip side was a national story about a female college athlete and abuse by male teammates. I choose to leave names out as she's been through enough. The abuse and the allegations were old stories but, for some reason, the national press was reviving it. ABC News asked me to get interviews with the athlete, her teammates and her coach. I told the assignment editor that there was very little chance that anyone involved was willing to weigh in publicly. I knew the Athletic Director and he was clear that the issue was closed.

She didn't care. She asked me to stake out the athlete's apartment. They paid me for three days of twiddling my thumbs then ended the gig. That same day NBC called and asked me to cover the same story. I told them that I'd already tried, and that it was a fool's errand. But they persisted. After three days they scolded me, angry that I didn't get the story that I told them that I couldn't get. I guess it made them feel important.

I cashed their check.

* * *

America's Most Wanted was tops on the trauma-tainment tour. There was a huge crime scene on Albuquerque's West Side. Some crazy serial killer had buried eleven women in a vacant field and the search for a suspect had grown cold. The vacant lot was one of the largest crime scenes in the country. The lot had been sold and was being prepared for development, an unfortunate complication.

To develop a virgin property, the developers will deploy bulldozers to dig up the dirt, then redistribute and pack it down for a hardened, stable building site. So earthmoving equipment had dug up the site, churned the dirt and re-deposited it, thus spreading the remains of eleven abandoned victims across the 100-acre site. The crimes remain unsolved with the prevailing wisdom assuming that the perpetrator is dead.

* * *

A second story we covered was called "Boots." An archer target-shooting in the desert happened upon the toe of a cowboy boot sticking out of the sand. One of his arrows had gone astray and landed by the boot. Digging with his hands, he quickly discovered that there was still a person in that boot, a dead woman. It was ten years since the woman had disappeared, so the case was ice cold. We shot the story and it went on air. The killer was captured in California less than a week from airing. When caught, he was still driving his victim's car. Criminals are stupid !

* * *

I first heard the term 'trauma-tainment' from a friend, a theater and speech professor, as we discussed black cinema. He was disturbed by the preponderance of films cashing in on slavery and the violence suffered by his ancestors. Trauma peddled as entertainment.

We agreed that the stories of our brutal history need to be told but there needs to be a balance, with an equal diet of tales of exceptionalism.

Mall Cop – No, Not That One

Mall Cop – A Low-Budget Disaster

Shot in 2004, *Mall Cop* was followed in 2009 by a much better film: *Paul Blart: Mall Cop*, a comedy starring Kevin James, best known for *The King of Queens* TV series. I met Kevin in Santa Fe before he hit it big, dressed in a chicken suit for a pizza commercial. The road to stardom… but I digress.

Mall Cop had an $800,000 budget, chump change for a Hollywood feature film. The director, David Greenspan, got the chance to direct his first feature after winning The Palm D'or for Best Short Film in 2001 at the Cannes Film Festival for a charming short film entitled *Bean Cake*. The Palm D'or is the top award at Cannes. You can see *Bean Cake* on YouTube: *Bean Cake* by David Greenspan.

Where do I start, hmmm, catering. A low-budget production can struggle to find quality vendors that will work within their budget. We suffered through five caterers, each worse than the last. Filmmakers are always fed breakfast, or a meal at the beginning of the shoot day. One late afternoon we arrived for a night shoot to find a tray filled with about seventy grilled cheese sandwiches. They were in a huge pile, having been cooked at least an hour before delivery, and had melted together in the heat to form one gigantic blob. We demurred. On most days the crew skipped the served meals, opting for Mickey D's or other fast-food choices nearby.

In the last week of production we were on location at night. Lunch was served after midnight so there weren't any better choices open. The caterer showed up with a vat of brown broth and half a baked potato for each of us. Oh my God ! The crew called it our *Schlindler's List* lunch.

Most of the film was shot in a mall scheduled for demolition. There were still a few stores hanging on but, to the camera's eye, it still looked full. Most of our shots portrayed the Mall Cop guarding the complex after closing time, alone. But there was a scene written to take place in a fountain with the actors cavorting around, nearly naked. We had shot all night and finally got to this scene at about seven AM. We didn't anticipate the arrival of a dozen 'mall walkers,' seniors getting their exercise in the safety and comfort of a heated mall. Yikes ! The grips quickly erected a wall of furniture blankets to hide the scene from the nice old ladies in gym shoes. Tragedy averted.

Then there was the pool scene. The script called for a pool at a low-rent apartment complex with the young stars in Frederick's of Hollywood undies. The location scout found a pool, but it was fall and the water temp was in the low 50s. The producer found a company that claimed that they could circulate the cold water through filters in their van and raise the temp. But it didn't work, so we had to muscle through in the cold pool.

The actors, a young man and two gals in their early 20s, were pissed. They got in the water but complained, loudly. They were right, it was freezing, but we had to 'make our day.' We pressed on until the actors threatened to walk off the film. I was the first AD with the responsibility of keeping the ball rolling. So I climbed in the pool with them, fully clothed, and we shot for hours. It's a miracle that we didn't die of pneumonia.

Mall Cop was regrettable but none of this was David's fault and he went on to direct numerous TV series.

Little League

It was the bottom of the eighth, two outs, with runners at 1st and 2nd. We were ahead 4 to 3 and we'd get out of the inning if I got the runner out at third. That's a lot of responsibility for a ten-year-old, and I was up to it. A line drive down the middle sent the players scrambling. The kid coming from second wasn't very big but he was barreling towards me like a runaway train. I saw the second baseman sling the ball to me for the out, straining to throw it with all of his might.

Then it all went into slow motion. Like a split screen, I could see the runner barreling towards me in the bottom frame and the ball winging its way to me past his head. Zzzzziing

I woke up with my head resting on third base. The ball had ripped through the pocket of my glove and smacked me in the nose, knocking me out cold. My Dad was the coach so I woke up looking at his worried face.

I think we lost the game.

Hands-Only CPR

At CNM the faculty attended mandatory training sessions each semester. There were always lists of workshops to attend but almost all of them were geared to academic subjects, lessons to be learned from a combination of textbooks and lectures. I was a filmmaking instructor. It was all hands on, no books. Each semester we'd produce five short films. That way the students learned the basics, starting with an idea through pre-production, production, and post-production. Get the first project done then rinse and repeat four times, with the students switching crew positions.

Looking at the workshop choices one semester, I picked a course in hands-only CPR, cardiopulmonary resuscitation. I had learned CPR decades earlier in the Boy Scouts but the methods had changed. Hands-only meant scrapping the idea of mouth-to-mouth breath support. So I took the course. The instructor was a paramedic and had a great presentation. At the end of the class I asked if my class could create a video to support his workshops. He jumped at the chance.

The project was perfect, combining a stand-up lecture with live-action demonstrations of regular people responding to heart attack victims. Local paramedics showed up with full gear for filming. We learned a lot. A side benefit of working in films is that you're exposed to all manner of products and professions as you go from one production to another.

During filming we had actors simulate their response to a heart attack victim. They apply CPR to keep the victim alive until paramedics arrive. But we questioned why the paramedics walked slowly to the scene with a gurney and medical bags. We all thought that they should be running in response to the emergency, but the instructor helped us understand that walking at a standard pace is policy since they could injure themselves while running and thus be unavailable to help the victim. The instructor also covered the warning signs of a heart attack so that you could recognize a symptom early and spring into action.

A year later I felt pressure in my chest late on a Thursday evening but discounted it as stress and went to bed. In the morning, Good Friday, I proceeded with my day until the symptom returned around noon. Thinking that it was acid indigestion I sought an over-the-counter remedy at a pharmacy. The pharmacist told me to sit down so that she could take my blood pressure. It was through the roof, 265 over 120. I was having a second heart attack in two days and completely ignored the warnings showcased in the video I'd directed. Duh ! I even drove myself to the hospital in the midst of the second attack. Double Duh !

In sort of a comic, or cosmic twist, I had the first attack during what Christians call Holy Week, with the first attack on Holy Thursday, the second on Good Friday, surgery to insert stints on Holy Saturday then released from the hospital on Easter Sunday. Go figure !

Props And Set Dressing –
The Art Department

The art department has a larger crew than most departments, comprising construction, painting, props and set dressing – all contributing to the 'look' of the picture. Accolades are showered on directors and actors but the story needs an environment suiting the time and the mood. I'm focusing here on props and set dressing.

The set dressers flesh out every scene with furniture, pictures on walls and tabletops, rugs, knick-knacks and collectibles, plus food items on kitchen shelves and sticky notes and magnets on the refrigerator, all relating to the characters, the mood, and the time period. First, the art director sketches a game plan complete with photo examples, then they send 'buyers' to find items fitting the scheme. Buyers focus their search in a few areas : retail stores, antique stores, flea markets, and thrift stores. In LA there are massive prop shops with substantial collections. In one prop shop I saw a dozen choices of old bikes, a half dozen coffins and three vintage gas pumps – and that was just the lobby.

Every semester when teaching college filmmakers, I'd take them on an art department tour, visiting antique stores, indoor flea markets and thrift stores. Generally, antique stores have items dating from the '60s and before, while flea markets tend towards newer fare including kids' toys from the '60s to present day, but not as precious. Thrift stores offer some of the same but in more worn condition, good for a lower-income household or hyper kids scenes.

I used to show the classes a vintage Mickey Mouse alarm clock, with a hammer striking two bells on top, that I found in an indoor flea market for $18 bucks. I opined that the same clock would cost over $75 bucks in an antique store. I shared the story with a friend and he responded that he collected clocks. I sold him the clock for my cost, $18 bucks. But he had the good sense to get the clock appraised. It would sell to a Disney collector for $800.

* * *

The prop master on *Breaking Bad* and *Better Call Saul,* Mark Hansen, was always prepared. His office looked like a yard sale had just blown in, with the floor, shelves and his desk covered with varied items. He had a semi-trailer packed with props for the show, complete with countless plastic bins filled to the brim, and a gun safe. When a director calls for a prop, it's customary to show them a few choices, that's why the bins are full. I was intrigued to see a bin marked 'clean trash.' Is that like military intelligence ? (ha, ha) Company logos are forbidden in the picture so clean trash is simply trash without logos – and *military intelligence saves lives !*

Mark has multiple trailers, with props appropriate to Westerns in one, modern day in another and so on. His assistant on BB and Saul, Trina Siopy, was usually on set. I interviewed her often for EPK videos. On BB episode 512, she outfitted Aaron Paul with a 'wire' to catch Walter White on tape admitting to a crime. The mic was taped to his chest. Between takes she removed the mic, pulling some hairs off Aaron's chest. She turned and joked to the camera that she was selling Aaron's hairs on Ebay.

 To see the video, go on YouTube to *Making of Breaking Bad Episode 512*.

Trina was elevated to Associate Producer on the final two seasons of *Better Call Saul.*

* * *

Some set dressing needs to be created. On *Suspect Zero* the film opens on a stream of rainwater gurgling down a trashy hillside. The camera tilts up to reveal a milk carton with the picture of a missing child. That carton had to be designed and printed, same with newspapers with headlines specific to the script.

A prop is any object that an actor handles. Often an actor will pick up a piece of set dressing like a candle stick. Now it's a prop and will be passed from the set dressing folks to the props department, ready for multiple takes and re-shoots. There's always an on-set dresser with the shooting crew during filming to adjust dressing for the frame. A props person is on set also to hand props to actors and retrieve them after the shot.

Weapons used by the actors are handled by the armorer. On smaller films and commercials, the props dept. handles the weapons and vehicles as well.

On stage, the props and set dressing departments each have a 'Gold Room' where they stash goodies that may be used on the set later. Sometimes a director will choose to replace a lamp on set due to its color or size and the on-set dresser will zip to the gold room to bring other choices. It's the same with props. On a medical show, the production might use up syringes or IV bags in a scene and they'll be replenished from the props gold room.

At the end of a season, the props and set dressing are boxed, stacked on pallets, wrapped in plastic and sent to storage. The set walls are carefully disassembled and marked for re-assembly for the next season. They also go to storage. Studio rentals cost $5,000 a day per stage for shoot days and half that for prep and wrap, plus electricity, so it's customary to clear the stage for rental to another production. Then bring it all back for the next 'season.'

Are We Responsible ?

Please don't mind me getting serious for a minute. Whenever there's a mass shooting some voices point to violent movies and video games as responsible. I'm not saying that. I am asking that the conversation happen within the industry. But the industry is a cash machine so I'm not holding my breath.

I think there's a difference regarding video games where you become an active player, killing without regard for consequence. Viewers watching TV shows and movies are passive participants. They're imagining. I question our responsibility there. Special effects and effects makeup have evolved to make wounds more realistic and scary. The marketing campaign for *Saving Private Ryan* stated that the battle scenes looked like the real thing, what the soldiers actually experienced. I get it, but it's not for me.

Having worked in the industry for three-plus decades makes me shy away from that realism. My son hounded me to watch *Yellowstone*. When I finally relented, I enjoyed the show but there was a scene with graphic gore in each of the first two episodes. Gore for the sake of gore. I realized that this was a convention that they'd follow in future episodes, like filming from the inside of the refrigerator to see someone open the door on *Breaking Bad*.

Plus, *Saving Private Ryan* was about real war compared to stories dreamed up by writers, producers and directors who hire effects artists to actualize their vision, all from the safety of their homes and offices. Regular Joe on the street doesn't enjoy that safety when a nut job decides to replicate something he saw.

The movie *Towering Inferno* made me afraid to ride elevators for ten years. Every time I stood in front of an elevator I'd 'see' an image of a person in flames falling out when the doors open, as depicted in the film. The graphic violence in *A Clockwork Orange* got to me, too. I love Stanley Kubrick's films but I couldn't watch this one again for ten years.

At present, I can't watch war films because my son is a Marine and I just don't need those images.

There's plenty of violence in books, too, but it's different when you see it in pictures. One of my favorite books is *In Cold Blood* by Truman Capote. Every time I see a classic white farmhouse fifty yards off the road, I'm reminded of the violent death of the family portrayed in the story. And there are a lot of old, white farmhouses where I live in Virginia. But I don't see a teenager's brains splattered on the wall like I'd see in a film. I guess I need to stick with *Willy Wonka* and *The Princess Bride* !

I admit that I'm overly cautious. I can't expect the industry to be aware of or sensitive to my needs. I can always vote with my feet. I just think that it's a discussion that's swept aside by polarized positions, possibly to society's detriment.

* * *

On the lighter side, I had a CAT scan today. When I mentioned my filmmaking past, the nurse shared a story of a patient from years past. It was the nurse's first responsibility to explain the procedure to each patient, but this woman stopped her, saying, "I know all about it, I watch *House* ?!"

Civil Disobedience

How'd you like to get handcuffed and carted away from an uninhabited, wind-swept desert location… on your 30th birthday.

There's a nuclear waste dump in Southern New Mexico called the WIPP site, the Waste Isolation Pilot Plant. The federal government dug a very deep hole into a massive, underground salt deposit, carving out caverns to store transuranic waste, low-level trash left over from nuclear weapons research and testing.

Tons of irradiated tools, clothing and other leftovers from the development, testing, and manufacture of nuclear weapons had piled up at various sites around the country. The government had hoped to dump the radioactive trash in the Yucca Mountain Nuclear Waste Repository, just 90 miles from Las Vegas, Nevada, but citizens and the state government put a halt to that effort.

Yucca Mountain was finally shut down after spending $11,000,000,000 on the failure. That's 11 billion in taxpayer cash, but who's counting ? The Yucca Mountain project was different, planned to store high-level radioactive waste.

So New Mexico got the call, and the citizens were pissed, reacting to this proposed plan not just to store the waste in a remote desert location, but to invite tens of thousands of shipments of radioactive waste on state roads and railways. Yikes times a million ! The pushback from the state environment department wasn't enough to stop it so a band of concerned citizens rose up.

After much chatter about legal strategies and protests, a small group chose to take direct action through civil disobedience at the site. There were 21 of us. You can call us hippies or radicals or whatever but the thought of sharing highways with nuclear waste transports was too much to let pass unchallenged.

The leaders of the group met with the local Sheriff in Carlsbad and settled on a plan. There was nothing at the location except a lonely sign announcing the 'future site of.' It was a barren stretch of desert. It was agreed that the Sheriff would draw a literal line in the sand and arrest us when we crossed over the line. It may seem silly, but the point of civil disobedience is to draw attention to an issue, and the Sheriff helped us in a way we never expected. They arrested the press along with the protestors ! Reporters had come to document the event but left in handcuffs. Our little protest in the desert made national news, a far greater splash than we'd anticipated. My parents in Philly saw me getting arrested on the nightly network news.

At the time, I was working as a cook at The Morning Glory Cafe and attending college at UNM. At the Cafe, I informed my boss of the event and offered that he should fire me if I was arrested, as I'd be unable to cover the schedule. That led to a nutty exchange with the Sheriff's deputies.

We crossed the line in three rows of seven. I was in the first row and was the first to be arrested. Some of the group sat down and demanded to be carried but I didn't see the point in that, so I was escorted to a folding table set up to process us. The deputy asked the usual questions: name, address, occupation and the like. When he asked my occupation, I answered 'unemployed' based on my agreement at the cafe. Then he asked if I had any tattoos or identifying scars. I responded that I have scars on both wrists and needle tracks on both arms. The deputy looked up at me in disgust. I could see the wheels turning in his head, judging me to be an unemployed, drug-addicted, suicidal hippie. But none of that was true.

You already know why I was unemployed. The scars on my wrists were from two bonehead accidents. I got the scar on my right wrist ten years earlier during my freshman year, and only year, at the University of Scranton in PA. Trying to force open a stuck window, I shattered the glass, resulting in a nasty gash. About eight years later, I was working as a grocery clerk on New Year's Eve, stocking the dairy department shelves. As I opened a case of butter with a box cutter, I turned my head to admire a gorgeous shopper and slashed my wrist. No suicidal tendencies at all. Life is too much fun !

The track marks on my arms were from dozens of times that I'd given blood (platelets) for hemophilia and leukemia patients. My dad had volunteered to give white cells and convinced me to join him. The process was more demanding than the typical twenty minutes where you donate a pint, sit for a few minutes to pass any lightheadedness, and get sent home with a juice box and a cookie.

No. We were donating white cells, and we were matched to individual patients. I was matched with a child in Boston. The donating process took two hours. Our blood was drawn from one arm then pumped through filters to gather the white cells, then the remaining red blood was returned into a vein in the other arm. Quite trippy. After extracting the white cells that I donated in Philly, the staff would package the bag of cells in a cooler and have it flown to Boston for a child that I'd been matched with.

Because we had the red cells returned to our bodies, we were able to donate weekly. But it left track marks and that was all the deputies saw. Why waste a good laugh explaining.

We were carted away in a Sheriff's bus with bars on the windows, protestors and journalists alike. Realizing their mistake, the sheriff released the journalists that day. The protestors were held overnight to face a judge in the morning. At a preliminary hearing the next day, the Judge set a trial date a few weeks later.

Sadly, in my opinion, some of our group had a martyr complex. We'd already made the news so the event was a success, but some of the leaders wanted more. They opted to hire a local, inexperienced attorney, and we were sentenced to ten days in the county jail plus a $250 fine each.

Returning to classes two weeks later, many of my classmates applauded the effort. The Chairman of the UNM Theater Department took up a collection to pay my fine. It was a 30th birthday to remember !

* * *

While incarcerated in the county jail, with 18 of us in a cell built to house eight, we were crowded together like mice. Of the 18 men, 12 of us were protestors and six were locals with varied offenses. One gent was a violent repeat offender, jailed this time for sex and violence on a minor teen girl. Let's call him Otto.

To pass the time we took turns sitting at a table with six metal seats bolted to the floor, writing letters and postcards. Suddenly, Otto started pounding on a fellow inmate, one of the locals, repeatedly punching him in the head from behind. I still don't know where I got the courage but I jumped between them and confronted Otto. He didn't take it kindly. He grabbed my jail jumpsuit with both hands, shoved me against the bars and grinned.

"I'm facing ten years when I get to court and smackin' you around will only add maybe a year, no big deal." As he released his grip I reached out and brushed his shoulders as if grooming a son on his way to the prom, a gesture straight out of an Adam Sandler comedy, but Otto smiled and let me walk away.

* * *

When we were released, I asked to speak with the Sheriff. His office was decorated like a comedy set, complete with a gigantic oak desk and a large bass mounted on the wall behind him, with a cigar dangling from its mouth. He told me that he sympathized with us, explaining that he had two adult sons, one who would have joined our protest, and the other a sailor on a nuclear sub.

He went on to share a story from his childhood. He grew up in a farming family and had regular chores, including feeding the horses before dawn. One morning he was walking to the barn in the dark, carrying two buckets of oats, when the 'world lit up.' Those were his words, the world lit up ! He dropped the buckets and ran to the house, scared to death.

His family farm was located on the far side of a mountain range separated from the White Sands Missile Range. It was the morning of July 6, 1945, and he'd just witnessed the explosion of the atomic bomb test at the Trinity site. Holy hell, this guy had a lot more experience with nuclear issues than all of us protestors combined.

* * *

There's always an upside to any experience – for me it was losing a pound a day in jail. Our meals were sparse and our 'fresh vegetable' at every meal was ketchup. Yummy, but not very filling. I was already tall and skinny but the loss of ten pounds left my pants pretty loose. So the deputies didn't notice that I was sneaking out with my orange jail jumpsuit stuffed down my pants. It was a fabulous Halloween costume the next year.

* * *

There are voices extolling the safety of nuclear power and the cleanliness of the process, a seemingly positive alternative to fossil fuels. But human error is always a factor. What about *Three Mile Island,* and *Chernobyl,* or *Fuck-you-shima* ?

Advocates pushed back, declaring that the WIPP site only handles low-level, slightly radioactive waste. But a few years ago, a technician at the Los Alamos National Labs made a mistake while packing a barrel of waste for shipment. It was common to add kitty litter to liquid waste to stabilize it, but the tech switched from inorganic clay litter to organic litter, causing a chemical reaction. The drum exploded.

The explosion spread the waste in the cavern, contaminating a large area and some of the workers. The entire site was shut down for two years to study and clean up the accident, costing taxpayers an additional $640 million. The LA times reported that the actual cost of the accident would approach $2 billion. More taxpayer money.

Doctors and Autopsies

The Night Shift

I've never been a fan of medical shows but I had the opportunity to work on *The Night Shift* and was duly impressed. The series follows a group of former Army field surgeons who return home to work the night shift in the emergency room at a San Antonio hospital. To add realism to their parts, the actors learned some basic medical practices. They could suture a wound on camera with help from the FX department.

One episode featured a woman transported to the ER following a car crash. She was nine months pregnant and the doctors had to perform an emergency C-section. The actress was fitted with a pregnant belly, and the realism extended to a fake placenta handled by the docs during the emergency birth. FX made a fake infant that looked very real. To enhance the reality, the director planned a handoff. The doctor 'caught' the fake baby and turned to hand it to a nurse, but he hid the action, like a quarterback on a bootleg hiding the ball behind his back.

The nurse pretends to take the fake baby but is already cradling a live infant and proceeds to show the mother that her baby is OK. That created a continuous take with no cuts. Great choreography.

* * *

Casting infants is tricky. As with twins, you need multiple babies to complete your shots. There were eight infants cast to play one child for the day, protected with their moms in a production office re-purposed as a nursery. Infants can only work on camera for twenty minutes in a shoot day, so swapping babies is necessary and tricky. The babies have to look similar. Some infants are born with lots of hair. My sons were bald for months after birth. The difference would be noticeable. And have you ever noticed in a film where a baby is much too large to have been birthed that day. Ouch, Mom !

Between takes the AD came to video village to speak with the director. She asked him to notice that the hair on the live baby didn't quite match the fake baby. He looked troubled and asked how the mistake had happened since they worked in prep to ensure a closer match. The AD responded that, due to a production delay, they'd had to cast a whole new set of infants since the original group had grown too big to look like they were born that day. The director accepted the reality and moved on.

* * *

Realizing that the stand-by babies were somewhere off set, I sought out the makeshift nursery. I'm always looking for a fresh angle for the EPK videos, so I grabbed my camera crew and headed to the nursery. Luckily, the head of casting stopped us in our tracks. Even though our shot wasn't part of the show, it would still count towards the allowable 20 minutes on camera. All of the babies would have to be excused for the day and production would be stuck without an infant for the birth scene.

The producer would have had my head. Close call.

* * *

The ER set for *The Night Shift* was impressive with room for eight patients separated by curtains. A real emergency room. The expansive set also included operating rooms, a CAT scan room, a nurses' station and a doctors' lounge, all completely dressed out. The production was spread across two huge stages, allowing for a very long hallway, perfect for doctors rushing a patient on a gurney to another part of the hospital. Set dressing rented tons of medical equipment for the set that was transported from LA in seventeen forty-foot trailers. Every room was packed with colorful bins holding fake medications, IV bags and everything needed for an emergency.

The nurses' station was dressed to look very active with charts and phones and sticky notes with scribbles that were changed for every script day, like would happen in real life. Exterior shots of the ER were filmed at the Lovelace Medical Center where my son, Keaton, was born.

Often filmmakers create side businesses that support production. It's standard practice, and a union rule, to have a medic on set at all times. The head medic in Albuquerque saw an opportunity and jumped on it. The show needed ambulances to transport patients in the story. So he bought a couple of ambulances that were being retired from service and rented them to the show. From then on the ambulances were housed at the studios and were repainted often to portray emergency services on films set in varied cities.

I'm still not particular to medical shows but I respect their realism.

Wombat

While studying for my bachelor's degree in Theater Arts I scored a job as a cook at The Morning Glory Cafe, just a block off campus. On my first day I was the lone cook, along with two waitresses and a dishwasher. I was 29 and the dishwasher looked to be 50 or older. He had wild grey and white hair and a totally out-of-control beard. The waitresses told me to stay away from him, saying that he mumbled incoherently all day. They told me his name was Wombat.

I can't ignore a fellow human, so I visited the dish room a few times with pots to be washed. It was a chance to be near him and hear what he was mumbling. It turned out that he was an accomplished Shakespearian actor preparing for an upcoming play. He was literally reciting Shakespeare the whole day. We became fast friends, sharing the love of Charlie Chaplin's comic antics and Frank Zappa's zany lyrics. WOW !

I forget which Shakespeare play he was in, but it was produced in Popejoy Hall, a 2,000-seat theatre on the UNM campus. Wombat was the best performer in the cast by far. He had grown his hair and beard to fit the role.

Judge not lest ye be judged !

Suspect Zero Autopsies

Many years later I was hired as an additional AD on the film *Suspect Zero* with Sir Ben Kingsley, Carrie Ann Moss and Aaron Eckhart. There's a lot of hoops to jump through to "prep" for film production. It takes months if not years to get all your ducks in a row before principal photography begins.

The plot of *Suspect Zero* revolves around serial killers. Ben Kingsley is off his rocker. He was a government agent made crazy learning remote viewing, seeing events before they happen. He used his vision to hunt and kill serial killers, a light rom-com….

Ben is pursued by FBI agents Aaron Eckhart and Carrie Ann Moss. So, young filmmaker, picture the FBI offices with binders, files and maps covering tables and desks where the agents sort through details. That would include photos.

If you're chasing a serial killer, you have evidence of past crimes, past murders. Bodies found abandoned in remote locations, decomposing. So before starting principal photography we needed to produce a stack of photos of dead women, evidence. A trail to follow.

I was charged with creating the photos in the autopsy rooms of New Mexico Medical Investigators in Albuquerque. Usually the art department sends set dressers to create the environment. But shooting in actual autopsy rooms shorted that process. These rooms are the real deal with all the equipment and props they use every day.

But where do you find women willing to strip naked for a photo ? Easy, you hire strippers. They're comfortable appearing in the nude. But these were abandoned bodies, so each woman spent hours in our makeup trailer being outfitted with cuts and bruises, evidence of abuse before their deaths.

The OMI docs had fun commenting on our 'dead bodies,' rating them on a scale of believability. They were very opinionated, and it was a fun exchange. It took a week to create photos of ten unfortunate victims. We did all of this while the docs continued their duties, receiving cadavers from the latest tragedies. And some of *them* didn't look real. One body showed up without a head; weird, didn't look real.

Side note : Strippers are people too. Don't judge. One woman was an elementary school teacher by day and a stripper at night, making cash to buy school supplies for her classroom.

Semi Runs Over The Audience – *Suspect Zero*

In *Suspect Zero* our heroes track a serial killer, but we don't get to see the killer's face until the final ten minutes of the story. Prior to that, we see a semi hauling a 40-foot trailer. Throughout the story, we see the truck roll past a marching band or a schoolyard, and you know that another child has been kidnapped and killed.

To intensify the audience's fear of the truck, we shot a scene where the semi drives directly at them, seemingly rolling right over them. One way to accomplish that would be to position the camera in the middle of the road and let the truck roll over it, sitting safely on the road as the truck passes over it. But the director and DP wanted a greater impact. They wanted the camera at the height of a human, creating the illusion that you were standing in the road and got creamed. So the camera needed to be as high as the top of the truck's radiator. Sounds dangerous, but possible.

One solution would be to use a 'crash box,' a metal box with the camera inside that can take the violent impact but still protect the camera. That's how they shot the scene in *Lethal Weapon II* when the bad guy's house crashes off a hillside and falls directly on the camera. After the take, the crew had to dig through the rubble to find the crash box and retrieve the shot footage.

But our DP had a better idea. Let's use a mirror and geometry. Again, this is Michael Chapman who shot *Raging Bull* and *The Fugitive*.

Michael selected a two-lane road in Moriarity, New Mexico, with local police securing the closed road. A gigantic mirror, eight feet by six feet, was propped up on the road at an angle. Then the camera was positioned safely off to the side of the road, at an angle relevant to the mirror.

The camera rolled and the truck was cued. We watched as the truck barreled forward and smashed through the mirror, a brilliant solution.

We had a second mirror standing by but didn't need it. The effect was accomplished on the first take. In the theater, the audience would experience the truck speeding directly at them.

I've mentioned the crew position PA before. It stands for production assistant on most sets, but a PA is sometimes used like a Pack Animal. The poor PAs had to clean up the glass from the broken mirror before we re-opened the road to traffic. Imagine how far the broken glass was spread after being smashed by a speeding semi.

Carrie-Anne Moss

Film sets can be dangerous for many reasons. There are electric cables and junction boxes spread across the production area regardless of size. I've worked on many sets where electricians laid out cables stretching a city block from the generator in order to deliver power to distant lights.

And weapons on set are an obvious danger that require diligence from the crew and cast in following protocol. But there are constant challenges born from production elements on locations used for a single day or a single shot, with design and construction elements that are safe, but challenging.

On *Suspect Zero*, Carrie-Anne Moss played an FBI agent tracking a serial killer. In one of the final scenes in the film, Carrie-Anne saves a young boy held captive by the killer in the refrigerator compartment of a tractor-trailer.

Prior to this scene the truck, driven by the serial killer, crashes in a desert ravine while being chased by Aaron Eckhart and Sir Ben Kingsley in an SUV. The truck and trailer roll on its side as it crashes into an arroyo (ditch). We shot the chase and crash on BLM* desert land near Mount Cabezon, about 30 miles from Albuquerque.

But the actual rescue scene was shot days later in a parking lot in town. A second identical trailer was positioned on its side, with the tail end raised to match the angle of the crashed rig in the arroyo.

Two cameras were positioned in the front end of the trailer, near where the boy was trapped, and Carrie-Anne was stationed on a raised platform, preparing to enter at the elevated rear doors. I was the second unit AD for the shot. I asked Carrie-Anne if she wanted a rehearsal and she demurred. She was scheduled to fly back to LA that day and wanted to get on with it.

My concern was that she might slip as she rushed down the incline on the sheet metal side of the trailer. She was wearing short heels consistent with her role. We rolled the cameras and I cued her to enter. Her feet were sure as she started down but I could see in her eyes that she was aware that stopping would be difficult. She proceeded like a pro, rushing with the urgency of the little boy's life.

There was only one solution – I'd have to catch her before she slammed into the front wall of the trailer, like players in the NFL who help a charging player stop when they rush out of bounds. Out of frame, I held out my arms showing that I was there for her.

Carrie-Anne crashed into me hard. I wrapped my arms around her as we stumbled a few steps and came to a safe stop. We shot the scene twice.

How many times on your job have you embraced a movie star as part of your job responsibilities, and gotten paid, not sued? Carrie-Anne was gracious and professional, willing to take risks to fully portray her character.

Sir Ben Kingsley

There's a special tradition when filming on Native American tribal lands in New Mexico. Often referred to as reservations and pueblos, they are sovereign territories governed by the tribes, with regulations specific to their land that must be respected. It's different than filming on all other properties in the country.

The production *Suspect Zero* was partially shot on the Zia reservation. Before we proceeded with our work, we were invited by the tribe to a ceremony led by a Medicine Man, blessing us and our endeavor. About 75 cast and crew members attended the ceremony. We gathered in a large circle. The Medicine Man was the only speaker, blessing us both in English and in his native language.

Directly across from me stood one of the film's stars, Sir Ben Kingsley, an Academy Award winner for his portrayal of Mahatma Gandhi.

Sir Ben stood with a female companion and a young boy, about four years old. As the ceremony progressed, the little boy got restless and started to wander. His caring mother followed him and they ended up a few steps behind Ben. As soon as he noticed, he stepped back to stand equal to them. It was an act of humility and caring, quite fitting for the occasion.

During production I was assigned to the second unit where we seldom have interactions with the leading actors. On two occasions I visited the first unit to get marching orders from the show's producer, Oscar winner Jonathan Sanger. On both occasions, standing face to face with Jonathan, I was treated to a shoulder massage. I turned to thank whoever was rubbing my shoulders… it was Sir Ben, a truly kind and warm man.

Breakfast At Tiffany's

Of all the iconic filming locations, the opening shots in *Breakfast at Tiffany's* with the empty NY streets is absolutely iconic, focusing on a lone taxi and ending on Audrey Hepburn at Tiffany's window, with a danish and coffee.

Before I die I want to replicate the scene, standing alone on a quiet Sunday morning with croissant and coffee. I'd wear pearls to complete the look but that may be risky in these judgmental times.

Breaking News : I'm planning a trip to NY before year's end to catch a coupla Broadway shows. I need to add Sunday morning at Tiffany's to my plans.

More Breaking News : I purchased a set of pearls at my sister, Sharyn's, church Bazaar and have a trip to NY planned for February.

Pediatric Oncology

Before the film biz exploded in Albuquerque, I was a welcome guest at the 'Q Studios,' now Netflix Studios.

I'd worked on numerous productions at the stages and was a filmmaking instructor at the community college, CNM. Every semester I'd take the students on a tour of the stages to inspire them. It's impressive to stand in an empty stage with 52-foot ceilings and big enough to build a hospital ward with room to spare. For five seasons, *Breaking Bad* built the interior of Walter White's house on a stage leaving enough space to build additional sets.

Occasionally we'd be invited to watch production. For the students it was a bridge from their dream of a film career to witnessing a major film in production. We were invited to watch filming on *Independence Day : Resurgence* and *Breaking Bad* – a real eye opener.

I'd often get calls from a producer or production coordinator looking for a PA, an office helper, or an intern for the camera department. It was a blessing to get aspiring young filmmakers their first set job.

But this call was different.

The activities coordinator in the Pediatric Oncology department at Presbyterian Hospital, Annie Lopez, had called the studio with a request and the studio forwarded the request to me. I'd never heard the words 'pediatric oncology' and I was about to find out. It means kids with cancer. I'm tearing up just repeating the words.

Annie was looking for a director to work with the kids creating a music video that they were a part of, shot in the halls and patient rooms where they were being treated.

So she called the studios, not realizing that a film studio is just a large, empty room that producers 'rent' to shoot their opus. So I got the call.

The idea was to have the young patients choose a song and then film them dancing and lip-synching in their cancer ward along with their doctors and nurses. It was a way to bring cheer to the otherwise gloomy business of their treatment.

I jumped at the chance for two reasons : 1) life is service and 2) it was an opportunity to take a young film crew out of the classroom and into a unique environment to experience the realities of a shoot day. The kids chose the song "We Could Be Heroes".

Along with the hospital staff, we assisted the kids in creating costumes and art cards with affirmations to lift their spirits. The lead Doctor wore a multi-colored tutu and a staffer in a motorized wheelchair was dressed in an Iron Man costume. The kids jumped and danced and howled with joy.

My favorite image was of a tiny five-year-old boy with big glasses and an oversized baseball cap ringing a gong with a mallet. Patients got to ring the gong to celebrate their victory over the disease. At five years old, this little boy had beaten cancer. He now had a healthy life ahead. Dammit, I'm tearing up again.

The nurses asked us to include a segment dedicated to kids who'd died recently in their care. They gathered in an outdoor play area, made heart symbols with their hands and released a bouquet of balloons. It's hard to hold a camera steady when you're crying. God bless the Nurses, Doctors and staff who make this their life's work. Heaven has a luxury suite awaiting each of them.

When the edit was finished we threw a party for the kids, their parents, and the hospital staff, complete with a catered dinner and a band at the Explora Children's Museum. A local vendor set up two huge flat screens and we watched the video multiple times to the delight of the kids and their families. The kids watched themselves dancing and singing, pictures of joy and health in the midst of their challenging situation.

For my CNM students it was an awakening. Shooting on location has its challenges but shooting in a hospital is unique. There are issues involving sterile environments as well as individual patient needs. The film students got first-hand experience with an issue larger than themselves and the need to respect clients, whoever they are.

A year later we returned to the hospital for a second go-round with a whole new crew of students. This time we filmed the families at the Rio Grande Zoo and Bio Park swaying to the Cat Steven's tune "If You Want To Sing Out". Again, we hosted a dinner to view the video with staff and families.

Out of respect for the kids and their families the videos aren't available for casual viewing.

Mo'Nique and Cloris Leachman

I was sent to interview actress Mo'Nique on the feature *Beerfest*. Mo'Nique is known primarily as a comedienne but she won a Best Supporting Actress Oscar for her dramatic performance in *Precious*.

She was funny and very personal in the short time we spent together. She drew me into her world, affectionately nicknaming me 'my Chollie.' Referring to her Oscar win, she voiced frustration with entertainment media. They claimed that she was a newcomer, a new fresh face. She bristled at that, saying she'd been a performer for the past twenty years.

She continued, saying that she'd been around long enough to have 'fuck you money,' the ability to turn down any engagement because she didn't need desperation cash, a freedom that eludes most talent.

* * *

Whenever I enter a set, I ask the ADs for a call sheet, the list of actors and crew working that day. To my surprise Cloris Leachman* was in the cast. I called the office in LA and asked if they wanted me to interview her as well. Sadly, the young assistant had never heard of her.

Cloris Leachman won a Best Supporting Actress Oscar for her role in *The Last Picture Show* in 1971. She was also a regular in Mel Brooks' films, playing Frau Blucher in

Young Frankenstein and Nurse Diesel in *High Anxiety.* Her TV credits include *Two and a Half Men, Malcolm in the Middle,* and *Mad About You.* Her IMDB profile lists 288 films and TV shows that she performed in. She worked until she passed at age 94.

The assignment desk wasn't interested in any footage of her, their loss. But that didn't deter me. I *HAD TO* spend time with her. We rolled the camera, knowing that the footage would be ignored. But who cares, it's Cloris Leachman. The interview lasted five or six minutes but Cloris wanted to chat some more. I was thrilled. We cut the camera and she talked for twenty minutes more, sharing set stories from various films.

We had gotten chummy enough that I felt OK asking her to repeat my favorite line of hers from *Young Frankenstein.* She stood up, switched to a German accent and delivered the line in character: "Stay close to the candles, the staircase CAN be treacherous." Of course, the gag was that the candles weren't lit. I read recently that the original line in the script read "…the staircase MAY be treacherous." By switching 'may' to 'can' she implied that someone had already fallen. A comic genius, even re-writing Mel Brooks.

I felt honored to watch her work on *Beerfest.* In one scene, she's sitting at a long picnic table in a crowded beer hall. Her character is a grandmother, Great Gam Gam, a simple role but not for Cloris. She's always creating.

The scene was straightforward. She was to take the hand of a younger man and pull him onto the dance floor while delivering a comic line. After numerous takes, the director opined that the scene wasn't working. Cloris turned to him, saying that the problem was that the line wasn't funny. I watched as the blood drained from the director's skull. A comedy icon was taking him to task. He had written the script with a partner who was also on set. They called for a break to work on the line. It was during that break that I met and chatted with her.

Returning to the scene, she repeated the newly written line. During the next eight takes she massaged the line until it was funny, a comic genius at work.

The young man she pulled onto the dance floor was an extra. Extras don't expect to have one-to-one experiences with the featured cast but here he was, sitting across from Cloris at the picnic table. He was tall and slender with a scraggly beard and a star was leading him by the hand.

On the last take, she chose not to take his hand and instead, reached out, gently tugged on his beard, and led him to the dance floor, beard in hand all the way. The extra looked like he'd collapse from fright at any moment. They got the shot.

Country Roads and Prison Yards

Randy Travis – *Christmas On The Pecos*

I was never a fan of country music. I swore by the old joke : What do country songs and divorce have in common ? Somebody's about to lose their trailer. Then I met Randy Travis.

I was approached by a friend from the industry and asked to coordinate a Christmas Concert and DVD for Randy. It was a project with a dual purpose: to create a Country Christmas Special DVD, and to promote tourism in Carlsbad, New Mexico. The Pecos River runs through Carlsbad and every Christmas the city sponsors boat tours, floating down the Pecos past mansions decorated for the holidays with zillions of lights and animated features. It was cold, but blankets and hot cocoa were provided for the guests' comfort. We rode the river, filming the decorated mansions for the DVD.

Carlsbad is way south of Albuquerque, near the Texas border to the East. It was world-famous for the Carlsbad Caverns, a series of caves discovered in 1898. The caverns were developed as a tourist attraction in 1924, allowing visitors to hike down 850 feet to the cave floor, past stalactites and stalagmites that had formed over centuries by rainwater slowly migrating through the surface ground.

The coordinator's job on a production is to handle details so the producer and director can focus on larger issues. But the producer was spinning tall tales to Randy's manager and she saw through it. Randy's manager was his then wife, Elizabeth, who had discovered him as a young talent.

The challenge was daunting. Starting with a concert in a 2,000-seat auditorium in a podunk city that had never hosted talent at this level, followed by a trip to the bottom of the caverns to record Randy and a forty-voice choir, performing "Rock of Ages" and "Silent Night" 850 feet underground.

I had worked on details for the show for a few weeks before traveling to Carlsbad to meet Randy and his band. They were on stage rehearsing. Randy and Elizabeth were charming.

The producer met us onstage and proceeded to spin tales to the Travis's, offering production choices that weren't possible. The most egregious was his plan to shoot in the Caverns in the morning and the concert that night. Not possible. I took Mrs. Travis aside and explained the issues. She asked me to take over the show as producer/director. She remained the Executive Producer.

I was a guest instructor in the film department at CNM, and friends with the lead film instructor at ENMU, Eastern New Mexico University. I saw this as a great teaching opportunity. We recruited thirty college students who were guided by four film professionals shooting nine cameras.

I knew that I'd want close-ups on the musicians for the video and I didn't want cameras on the stage, blocking the audience, so I asked Randy and the band to do a full dress rehearsal in the afternoon before that evening's show.

All nine cameras shot the rehearsal, roaming the stage and giving us closeups of the musicians and extreme closeups on their instruments; fingers plucking a mandolin, drumsticks striking drums and cymbals. It was a good idea. During the evening show the cameras were positioned for wider shots with all of the cameras either off-stage or side-stage. With nine cameras shooting the two 'shows' we had 18 different angles to cut to at every second of every song for the DVD.

Randy was spectacular. The crowd was thrilled to be there and responded enthusiastically. My favorite part of the show had Randy reading the classic story *The Christmas Guest*.

In the story, an old cobbler named Conrad dreams that he will be granted his greatest wish: the Lord will come to visit him on Christmas Day. So he sat and waited for His arrival. Meanwhile, Conrad's Christmas is interrupted three times by weary travelers, whom he helps as he waits for his Lord to come. At midnight, frustrated, he prays again, asking the Lord why he had denied his wish. The Lord reveals to him that, indeed, he had come. He was the beggar, the distraught woman and the lost child who had come to his door, and Conrad had helped each of them and, by doing so, had received the Lord.

We lowered the lights on the stage with a special on Randy, sitting on a stool and accompanied by a guitar and mandolin. Midway through the story I had the crew sprinkle 'snow' on him from the rafters. The audience was mesmerized. At the story's end, Randy lowered his head, humbled by the story. The audience rose up in a wave, showering him with a long, standing ovation.

That was in December, perfect for Christmas. Then in March, we returned to shoot in the caverns. I enlisted a choir from a Carlsbad church to join the production, but they refused to rehearse or even meet Randy's music director prior to filming. The choir director claimed that his choir was good enough to perform without a rehearsal. I recruited a different choir.

On the day, the crew carried equipment on elevators to the bottom of the caverns, 850 feet underground. Once we exited the elevator the crew humped equipment on narrow trails to the shooting location in 'the big room.' The Park Rangers alerted us to the delicate nature of the millions of bats that made the caverns their home. They informed us that the female bats were pregnant and had to escape into the night to feed, but they'd stay put if there was too much light, confusing and starving them. So the crew used miner headlamps to negotiate the trails to the big room, carrying film equipment.

We shot with nine cameras in the caverns and added a long 'jib arm,' a crane with a camera mounted on the arm about twenty feet long, good for sweeping pans. Randy was alone, playing his acoustic guitar without his band, and backed by a forty-voice choir. I directed the production and was joined by Randy's music director from Nashville. We hired a company from Denver to record sound. Elizabeth and I stood close by, out of frame. The big room is 4,000 ft long, 625 ft wide, and 255 ft high at its highest point. BIG ! The acoustics were amazing !

We started with "Silent Night". At the end of the first take, the final note hung in the air for a lifetime, at least 20 seconds. I finally called cut but the music director squawked on the radio, asking that he be allowed to call the cut since the note continued to ring even longer. It was magical, beautiful, overwhelming ! During a take of "Silent Night" Mrs. Travis whispered in my ear : "It feels like we're in Heaven."

The DVD is titled *Randy Travis – Christmas on the Pecos*. I just checked Amazon to see if it was still available. It is, but it's expensive and rare.

 Many of the songs from the DVD are on my Youtube channel : https://www.youtube.com/ @chuckiedidit-sc3rm

* * *

Side note: Carlsbad Caverns is a National Park. The Rangers were concerned that if they opened the site for one video they'd have to allow anyone who asked. Can you imagine Ozzie Osbourne biting a bat in half in this stellar environment ? So they drew up a contract *inviting* Randy to become a spokesperson for the caverns, with his voice on the little recorders that visitors carry on their hike.

* * *

In the year following the show, I visited Randy and Elizabeth in their Santa Fe home. Elizabeth had created an amazing kitchen for her love of cooking. Randy had a large room equipped with lots of exercise equipment. There was a sitting area to the side with four chairs. Next to Randy's favorite chair, I noticed his Bible on a side table. I've known friends who used sticky notes to mark favored passages. Randy's bible had at least a hundred passages marked.

* * *

During the show we sprinkled snow on the band, using large tumblers and fans on scaffolding from both sides of the stage. Because we ran the show twice, I knew that we'd have to clean the snow out of Randy's hair at a certain point in the concert to avoid a problem in the edit. Randy had a great hairstylist named Mr. P., Philip Ivey, who had been with him since the film *Black Dog.* Mr. P is a big man, towering over Randy, and he's demonstrably gay.

We stopped the show to allow Mr. P and a helper to come on stage and blow the snow out of the band's hair. Carlsbad is just 40 miles from the Mexican border. It's very south and a bit redneck. I was concerned about what the crowd's reaction would be to Mr. P. Happily, the crowd cheered his flair as he tousled Randy's hair. Randy stepped to the mic and introduced him to the crowd, drawing a resounding cheer. He told them that Mr. P had won an Oscar for hairstyling on *Driving Miss Daisy*. The moment was such a hit that I stopped the show again a few songs later for Mr. P to make a second appearance.

* * *

The day after the show I was treated like a celebrity, the director who brought a national star to their little city. I was paraded around town by a city councilman. He gave me a tour of the important sites and businesses in Carlsbad. Our last stop was the offices for the WIPP site, the nuclear waste caves.

He drove to the corporate headquarters, a four-story modern building only ten years old, where he introduced me to the top execs running the project. WIPP is the underground series of caverns carved deep into salt beds in Southeastern New Mexico, where the government stores transuranic nuclear waste, and where I was arrested and jailed.

Hearing that I was a filmmaker, one of the execs asked if I would shoot a new film detailing the waste site. They had a film already, but the information was dated. She told me that I'd have full access, traveling 2,000 feet underground into the ancient salt bed.

The wheels in my head were spinning, here was a chance to get footage that I could pass on to the opposition. She had no idea that I had been arrested at the site years before. I drove back to Albuquerque mulling over the opportunity. I decided to go for it and called the exec to plan the job. But when I asked how much I'd be paid for the work she responded that she hoped that I'd be willing to do it as a volunteer. Her company had a 10-year contract with a $3 billion budget, and she wanted me to volunteer ? I thanked her and declined.

* * *

There were two objectives for the concert : 1) attracting tourists to Carlsbad, and 2) creating a concert video with special features to continue drawing tourists to the town and to the caverns.

The edit took the better part of a year. I had covered the show from every angle, with nine cameras shooting two shows. That meant that for any moment in the show there were 18 camera angles to choose from – wide shots, closeups, and tracking crane shots.

Twice during the edit I met with Elizabeth Travis at Tomasita's Santa Fe New Mexican restaurant, a favorite of hers and Randy's. Due to her celebrity, we were seated in a private dining room where the chef approached and asked Elizabeth what she'd like to eat. Forget looking at a menu, he'd prepare anything she pleased. Randy and Elizabeth were staunch Republicans, so Elizabeth shared her discomfort with me over the name of the room. It's The Hillary Clinton dining room.

The food was fantastic.

Adam Sandler – *The Longest Yard*

There's a prison outside of Santa Fe, the New Mexico State Penitentiary, the site of the most violent prison riot in US history. The inmates took control of the prison, holding 12 officers hostage and killing 33 fellow inmates. It was 1980 and the stain on the state lingered.

Jump forward some years and the State Government decided they wanted the prison gone. But how to do it ? It was rumored that NM offered the prison to Hollywood, hoping that it would be blown up as part of a film. But a prison built to house the most dangerous criminals in the state is a hardened shell, not easy to blow up.

So NM changed their tune, offering the site as a filming location. Coupled with generous tax rebates from the state, the prison location attracted the feature *The Longest Yard*, the 2005 remake. Prison inmates form a ragtag football team to challenge the guards with Adam Sandler as quarterback.

The cast was packed with stars: Adam Sandler, Chris Rock, Nelly, Nick Turturo, James Cromwell, and the star of the original 1974 film, Burt Reynolds. Tracie Morgan joined the cast along with NFL players Terry Crews and Michel Irvin and the always hilarious Cloris Leachman.

I was assigned to interview Adam Sandler. We talked numerous times during camera setups. I was surprised by his focus. He's a serious businessman, only dipping into his comic self when the camera was rolling. During any such assignment we shoot lots of B-roll to act as a visual base for the interview. B-roll are shots of the cast and production without dialogue, usually accompanied by a voice over narrator.

Adam's character is a star NFL quarterback who is charged with shaving points to throw a game. He goes bananas, wrecking a high-ticket sports car at the end of a wild police chase.

Prior to the formal, sit-down interview, I wanted B-roll shots of Adam throwing the football as if he was warming up. I had read many accounts of Adam's generous spirit from fellow actors and the public. The cast was taking a break during a camera setup so I asked Adam if we could get a shot of him throwing the ball. He graciously agreed. My camera operator focused on Adam as he threw the ball to me for a few minutes to get the footage. Yep – once again I'm getting paid to 'play' with a movie star. What a great career !

Later in the day we were ready for the sit-down, a formal interview with a bonafide comedian who doesn't act comically when not on set, a challenge. To guarantee some comic moments, I invited Chris Rock to join Adam for the interview. Sweet Jesus, it worked. Chris is the opposite of Adam, always kidding around, every moment a chance for levity. He brought out Adam's light side, cracking him up with zany comments. Adam couldn't help but laugh. The interview was a hit.

Tina Fey

Tina Fey has been an endless source of inspiration for me. Her book *Bossypants* is great fun, filled with stories from the sets of *Saturday Night Live* and *30 Rock*, plus pearls of wisdom from her personal experiences as a writer and performer. As a college instructor, I used examples of her career arc to inspire my film students.

Plus, it inspired me to write this book.

In *Bossypants*, Tina reveals a personal strategy. When faced with career decisions that seem daunting, she simply says "YES." She recalls that she was nervous in her first meeting with Lorne Michaels, she wasn't sure that she was ready for SNL. But he offered her a spot on the writing team and she said YES. When Lorne offered her the head writer's job, she was again faced with a challenge she was unsure of, and she said YES. And she said YES when offered a deal by NBC to create her own show, resulting in the hit, *30 Rock*. I often turn to Tina's career journey to inspire young students to take a chance, to feed their passion and go for it, full speed ahead.

An additional treat from *Bossypants* is hearing Tina's take on Lorne Michaels as the head honcho and the lessons she learned from his leadership. In one instance, she relates his calm approach to impending problems. Rather than make a snap decision, it was Lorne's practice to take a beat and wait for an answer to reveal itself.

He was wise and patient, ready to rein in 'creatives' who were spinning their wheels. She called it 'policing enthusiasm.' She cites an example where a script calls for a bran muffin on a white plate, but the props department delivers a bran cake shaped like Santa's face on a silver platter, thinking it would be funny. But, since the character is Jewish, Santa is inappropriate, and the metal tray causes a glare for the camera. Better to stick with the muffin on a plain plate. Policing enthusiasm.

I dog-eared that reference and so many others in her book, great examples of production challenges for aspiring filmmakers. *Bossypants* is available on Amazon and wherever great books are sold.

I had an opportunity to meet Tina during the filming of *Whiskey, Tango, Foxtrot* in New Mexico. There was an office location in the script and production conveniently chose to shoot in a UNM building situated next to the Albuquerque

Studios. I had an office on the top floor and taught film students in the 'studio' on the ground floor. I could have dropped by, innocently, to get something from my office, but, it's accepted practice in the industry culture that we treat actors as teammates, never asking for an autograph or fawning with admiration.

But, wait – Tina graduated from Upper Darby High School, just a stone's throw from my high school, Monsignor Bonner, in suburban Philly – surely she'd want to know that ??? Hardly. Tina didn't need me bugging her, she was working. I went on with my day.

The Sky Is Filled with Stars

Over three decades I was fortunate to meet and work with so many stars. Depending on your position on the crew, you may have regular contact with them or never meet them at all. Some passing contacts stand out :

Keith Carradine – Keith was in Santa Fe shooting a western. Everyone on the set was unhappy. I was only there for a day to interview the cast and I don't remember the title of the film or if it was ever released. But Keith was not thrilled to have to sit for an interview.

I always did my homework, researching the background of any actor that I was sent to interview. I wanted to have some instance in the actor's life or career to lighten the mood if the interview went south. IMDB has made research easy. With Keith, it paid off. One of my favorite films is the classic *Captains Courageous*. Shot in 1937, the cast included Spencer Tracy, Lionel Barrymore and Keith's father, John Carradine. It was my ace in the hole.

Keith sat to the side, waiting for his turn in front of the camera. I could see his impatience and had to get past it, so I mentioned that I loved his father's performance in the classic film. His face lit up. "Long Jack," he exclaimed, his father's character name. He spoke enthusiastically of his father and his role in the film. We bonded over tales of his dad and the interview went well.

See *Captains Courageous*, it's a must for any growing boy. It's a true 'coming of age' tale from the book by Rudyard Kipling. Spencer Tracy won his first Best Actor Oscar for the role of a humble Portuguese fisherman.

* * *

Giancarlo Esposito – You know Jean Carlo from *Breaking Bad*, *Better Call Saul*, *The Usual Suspects*, and more recently in *The Mandalorian*. Giancarlo is a very centered and spiritual gentleman. I interviewed him on *Better Call Saul* but the pace of production didn't leave time for small talk. I learned that the industry has mispronounced his name for years, thinking that he's Hispanic. In fact he's Italian. His full name is Giancarlo Giuseppe Alessandro Esposito. Check out his appearance in Spike Lee's films *School Daze* and *Do The Right Thing*.

* * *

Wesley Snipes – I was sent to interview Wesley during the pilot episode of the TV show *The Player*. The pilot was shot in Albuquerque but production moved to Las Vegas for the duration, needing shots of The Strip.

On many productions my crew was isolated from the shooting set, waiting for the ADs to grant us a few moments with the stars. On *The Player*, we set up in a vacant storefront nearby and received regular updates from the AD crew about Wesley's availability. Waiting, waiting, eating. Finally, at wrap, the AD told us that Wesley preferred to be interviewed the next day. No problem. We scored an extra payday.

Sometimes an actor will choose not to be interviewed at all. Kim Bassinger starred in *Elvis Has Left The Building* but declined to sit for an interview. Instead, I had a ball chatting with John Corbett and Denise Richards.

* * *

Frank Zappa – before entering the film industry I earned a few bucks as a photographer with contracts to shoot music acts playing locally. Gigs included photos of *The Police (Sting), The Isley Brothers, Boston, Ella Fitzgerald* and many more. But my favorite was Frank Zappa.

Frank's band was an anomaly, humble and professional. While other bands drank heavily and snorted whatever backstage, Frank's crew was different. There were no drugs or alcohol backstage or anywhere else. While every other band had minions carrying their instruments and wardrobes, Frank's bandmates took care of themselves. Quite humble. Not what you might expect if you listened to their music. Their music was out there and I was a fan. Check out his hit song "Cosmic Debris".

The second time I photographed a Zappa concert the vibe was tense. The first time I shot from the front of the audience and from side stage with no interruption. This time I wasn't allowed anywhere near the stage.

Frank had a cast on his leg, the result of a run-in with a jealous boyfriend in Europe. Apparently some guy got annoyed by his girlfriend's crush on Frank. He rushed the stage and tossed Zappa into the orchestra pit.

Consequently, for this show, he had added a bouncer, a large man with a blackjack neatly clipped on the back of his collar. He was serious business, and we danced. Whenever I got near the stage he'd jump down and chase me. But he couldn't go far. He had to stay close to Frank for protection. So I'd retreat until he got back on stage and weasel my way back to the front of the crowd.

If you're a Zappa fan don't miss his son, Dweezil, in concert. He's an amazing guitarist like his dad. And he wisely hired a singer to belt out Frank's lyrics.

The Toll Booth

1971 – Living in a hippie commune was fun. We had many adventures. One Saturday we drove from Boston south through Connecticut. The freeway was a toll road with booths inconveniently popping up every dozen miles. God knows they needed another quarter. But their plan backfired.

After dutifully surrendering numerous quarters, we pulled up to a broken booth. The basket was filled with quarters that hadn't gotten sucked into the machine's bloated belly. We chose not to add our quarter to the mess and drove away laughing.

A mile or so later we re-considered. We did a loop, getting off at the next exit and re-entering the highway in the opposite direction. At the next exit we completed the loop, entering the freeway going south again to get to the broken booth. We stopped and cleaned out the basket. The pile of quarters totaled $125 bucks. Eureka !

To celebrate, we treated ourselves to a sumptuous lunch. Picture four skinny, vegetarian hippies in a booth ordering everything on the menu, literally everything. The bill came to $100 and we paid with the quarters, leaving a $25 tip, also in quarters.

The waitress rolled her eyes… hippies !?

The Ninja Bandit

Criminals are stupid ! At the most elementary level it's stupid to think that you can get away with just about anything anymore. Do the crime and do the time. But there are standouts even amongst the criminal class.

Enter Matt Griffin.

Matt Griffin was an Albuquerque police officer convicted of robbing five banks and murdering a security guard in 1989. Investigators called Griffin the Ninja Bandit because he dressed in black from head to toe during the robberies. I was hired to produce a re-enactment of Griffin's crimes and capture.

On five occasions Griffin had entered banks dressed in all black. He'd rush in, jump up on the counter, and threaten the tellers with an automatic weapon. When investigators finally zeroed in on him as the suspect, they found evidence of the crimes in a closet in his home and in the trunk of his car. Stupid ! You'd think a police officer would be a bit more careful about hiding his crime. Duh !

In staging the re-enactment, I got to work with numerous APD officers. It was great fun, like filming an action flick but with real law enforcement. As always, I had a camera crew documenting the scenes, but it's a filmmaker's challenge to find unique ways to capture the action.

I met with the managers at two banks less than a mile from my house. I had accounts in one of them. I wanted to place a camera at ceiling level, looking down on the scene as if shot from a security camera. Then it dawned on me to simply use the bank's own cameras to record the scene. Imagine asking a bank manager to allow access to their security system. So I played the cop card, guaranteeing that I was working with local law enforcement and that officers would be on scene during filming. They both agreed.

The footage was priceless, partly because the camera angle was perfect and partly due to the grainy image created by low-resolution security cameras. It worked like a charm.

Griffin didn't stop getting into trouble, even after he was convicted and locked up. Although he was housed in maximum security, he continued to defy the system, slashing a guard's face with a razor. I still wonder how he did it, but the story goes that he was escorted by a guard to a medical office in the prison, slashing his face with a razor that he had swallowed, then coughed up at the right moment.

Somehow Griffin extracted a tiny blade from a safety razor, attached dental floss to the razor on one end and tied the loose end around his tooth. Then, at a convenient moment, he regurgitated the razor and slashed the guard. How the hell is that possible ?!

Guards responding to the scene subdued him, but that wasn't the end of it. Griffin sued the state claiming that the guards had kicked and punched him during the takedown.

The state settled, awarding Griffin $19,500. Cigarette money for life. Preposterous !

Japan's Bruce Springsteen

Shogo Hamada and "The Work Song"

In the film biz you're either in the union or you're an independent contractor, constantly looking for your next gig. Your reputation precedes you, and jobs come from varied sources.

I got a call from a Japanese producer based in LA. She was coming to New Mexico to film part of a documentary, a TV broadcast for the NHK, Japan's NPR. She said that the show was a fluff piece about a musician named Shogo Hamada. She called him the Japanese Bruce Springsteen.

HMMMMMM, what does that mean? I'd never heard of the guy so I envisioned a fabulous musician playing in small joints like Bruce did in the beginning in Asbury Park, New Jersey.

I went to the Albuquerque Airport to greet Mr. Hamada and his film crew. They were quite humble, carrying their own luggage, no roadies. Keaton was with me, about

9 years old. Mr. Hamada and his DP bowed in respect to Keaton and myself. These guys weren't like American rock stars at all. At home that night Keaton made a mix tape of his favorite music and asked me to give it to Mr. Hamada the next day. So cute !

On the first day we shot at Ghost Ranch in Abiquiu, New Mexico, famous for painter Georgia O'Keefe. As AD on the shoot, I called lunch midday. It's customary on American sets to invite the actors and DP to lunch first so they can eat and have time for short meetings before returning to set. I broke Mr. Hamada and the DP first, but they humbly insisted that they would sit and eat when their whole crew was with them. Incredible respect.

At lunch I walked off to a hill overlooking the mountains from Georgia's paintings, a moment alone and away from the hustle. I ALWAYS have a song in my heart, so I started singing "The Work Song" made famous by Nina Simone :

Breakin' rocks out here on a chain gang,
Breakin' rocks and serving my time.
Breakin' rocks out here on a chain gang,
'Cause you done convicted me of crime.
Hold it steady right there while I hit it,
Well, I reckon that ought to get it.
Been workin' and workin',
But, I still got so terribly far to go.

Mr. Hamada snuck up behind me and joined in. A duet on a lonely hilltop. He didn't speak much English but he knew the lyrics and we crooned together. We bonded in the moment. I called him Shogo from then on. The next day we filmed him singing and playing an acoustic guitar in a classic Santa Fe patio. He was really good.

At the end of the day, I mentioned that Keaton had made him a mix tape, not expecting to give it to him. He insisted and took it back to the hotel. The next day he had notes about the song choices for Keaton, delivered through an interpreter. What a sweetheart.

A couple months later I received a VHS copy of the documentary. Christ on a cracker ! There was footage of his concerts in 70,000-seat arenas. No corner bars for this guy ! The hour-long video featured lots of concert clips and interviews. The boys and I played the tape over and over, enjoying the music and the interview segments, all in Japanese.

Months later a package arrived from Japan, Christmas presents from Shogo to my boys. It was all concert swag, but who cares: T-shirts, hats and beach towels, presents from a bona fide Japanese rock star. We use both of the Shogo Hamada beach towels to this day.

Bumps in the Road

The Campaign Trail

During the 2004 presidential election I was sent to interview Martin Sheen as he stumped for John Kerry. The interview was originally scheduled during a campaign stop at The Cities of Gold Casino in Pojoaque, New Mexico, North of Santa Fe.

My crew and I arrived on time and security was loose, but Kerry's campaign manager rushed Mr. Sheen and Senator Kerry away, heading for another campaign stop on the plaza in Santa Fe. We packed up our equipment and raced to meet them there. We knew that the plaza would be packed and parking nearby would be tight, so we grabbed the first spot we found a few blocks away. I ran ahead to secure a spot for our camera, while the three-man crew gathered the equipment and followed a few minutes behind.

There were barricades and armed officers restricting access to the plaza. I approached alone and was stopped by the officers. I had no press credentials, the kind that hang from a lanyard, but the officers took my word for it and let me through. It's a good thing I'm not a terrorist.

Governor Richardson joined Kerry and Sheen on a portable stage, and they took turns speechifying and riling up the crowd. Sadly, we never got the interview as they were once again whisked away to another event. Too bad, I've always admired Sheen's work and had worked with his sons Charlie and Emilio in the past, but it wasn't in the cards that day.

Let's Get A Boy's Band !?

When Keaton was 12, he was cast in a commercial for the Coronado Mall dressed like a rockstar and playing a clarinet. The 30-second spot features 2 mall managers looking for a hook to draw in more customers. One of the guys recommends that they hire a boy's band for a show in the mall's atrium, thinking of the boy group NSYNC. But he wasn't quite clear, leading his partner to simply hire a boy who's in a middle school band. Comedy ensued.

Production assembled a stage with speakers on stands and lined up about fifty folding chairs for an expected audience. Keaton stood on the stage, alone, squeezing out discordant notes to the delight of two old ladies in the front row. A snoring senior in the back completed the audience of empty chairs.

Actually, Keaton doesn't play the clarinet. The first chair clarinetist from the New Mexico Symphony stood out of frame, playing the horrible, screeching tune. Somebody had the dumb idea to have one of the old ladies throw her bra on the stage. The art department showed up with a prop bra with the biggest cups I've ever seen. On the first throw, one of the cups landed on Keaton's head. We were happy that the gag didn't make the cut.

Every Problem Has A Solution !

For fifteen years I was a college instructor, teaching filmmaking to rising young talent. I regularly stressed that they had to think creatively when faced with a production issue. On a shoot day, you have only so many hours to get your shots before the sun sets. And time is money !

Melissa Bernstein, a producer on *Breaking Bad* and *Better Call Saul* used the phrase 'work arounds' to denote a strategy to move past an obstacle and complete the day. But creative thinking is an acquired talent. It was funny to watch students freeze when challenged. I shared my process; start with a call to whoever might have the answer and, if they don't, ask them who they would call. There's always an answer. I was pretty good at working through impediments, even a couple of times when my efforts were for naught.

On *Young Guns II*, I started in the production office, taking calls and solving problems. I wasn't on the shooting crew yet. The producer called from location and asked where we'd get a helicopter to lift an injured horse out of a canyon. I started by calling a helicopter service that we used for overhead shots, but their birds couldn't handle the weight. They suggested that I call the New Mexico National Guard. Again, no luck, but the National Guard suggested the Army.

I skipped a step and called the Pentagon directly since time was a factor. It still took a while. I was transferred a few times until, finally, I reached an officer who heard the problem and was willing to help. He gave me his direct number and told me to get the location of the canyon and call back. He guaranteed that he could have a heavy lift chopper deployed.

I hung up and called the producer on his cell. He was pleased that I had an answer and confessed that he hadn't been quite clear. There wasn't an injured horse, he just wanted a contact in case. We didn't need it, but I'd solved the problem.

* * *

On the film *Suspect Zero*, I was an AD on the second unit, planning for a chase scene with Aaron Eckhart and Sir Ben Kingsley in an SUV, chasing a serial killer driving a semi with a 40-foot trailer. Both vehicles crash at the end of the chase. The director chose a dirt road on BLM land

and I started to draw up a location agreement for the road. BLM management informed me that there was a natural gas pipeline under the road and needed us to ensure that it wouldn't be damaged. OK. How do you harden an already rock-hard dirt road against damage ?

Some years before, I'd seen a video of Navy Seabees, United States Naval Construction Battalions, building airstrips in remote locations in less than a day. There's not much Navy presence in New Mexico, so I called the Kirtland Air Force Base. They were quick with a positive response, excited at the prospect of working on a film. They invited me to the base to see how they could help.

To build a temporary runway, they used huge metal mats, like the old metal doormats that were good for scraping crud off your shoes. But these mats were huge, requiring an oversized forklift to place them. I returned to the producer with the issue solved only to be told that the director had changed his mind and chose another road.

I don't mind chasing my tail when I'm getting paid.

Tragedy on the Set of *Rust*

The death of Cinematographer Halyna Hutchins on the set of the film *Rust* was a tragedy. I believe that news reports of that day's events exacerbated the public's confusion.

*** Please note *** I was not on set and I have no first-hand knowledge. I wasn't there, but I know how sets work. I worked on numerous films and commercial productions on The Bonanza Creek Ranch where the tragedy occurred.

There's a problem with assigning a reporter to cover the story who has little knowledge of the day-to-day best practices that ensure safety for the cast and crew. Add to that a trend to hire fresh writing talent at salaries lower than their experienced counterparts and details get missed.

I read every article I could find on the tragedy and watched scores of news reports on network broadcasts and cable news. There were huge holes in the reporting, adding to the confusion. So, I'm reading between the lines.

Why would Alec Baldwin point a gun at a crew member ? He didn't. He was pointing it at the camera. Then why were the cinematographer and director so close to the camera ?

Film sets have wireless monitors for the director and cinematographer to view at some distance from the camera. There are monitors at video village* and small monitors on stands closer to the set but clear of the action. Those monitors are placed and controlled by the camera assistants.

Then why weren't Halyna and the director, Joel Souza, using monitors at a safe distance ?

Let's look at contributing factors:

A): The day before the tragedy the union camera crew walked off the production citing safety concerns and pay issues. They were replaced the next day by a non-union crew, new to the team.

B): The incident happened just after the lunch break.

C): It takes a good fifteen minutes after lunch for the crew to be back to full strength and ready to shoot.

D): The director, cinematographer and assistant director are often the first back on set, solving issues while the crew returns.

Halyna and director Joel Souza were back on set, lining up a shot. They wanted to be sure that they could see the gun that Baldwin would draw in the scene. Often an action is obscured by items in the background, even by the actor or their wardrobe. They wanted to be certain that the action was clearly portrayed and that the gun was clearly visible.

Adding A, B, C, and D, and I'm assuming that the off-set monitors had not been turned on yet by the camera crew returning from lunch. So Halyna and Joel huddled by the camera, looking at the tiny video screen on the back or on its side. That put them directly in the line of fire. I believe that was the set of factors that made the tragedy possible.

There were other issues that had to do with the individual responsibilities of the set armorer and the AD, but I'd rather not get sued so I'll leave that alone.

I've worked on dozens of productions with firearms without incident. Check out the scene in the final season of *Breaking Bad* where Uncle Jack and his criminal gang face off with DEA agent Hank Schrader and Agent Gomez in the desert. There were at least 8 firearms of different types in a violent exchange, and no one was hurt. I was there and interviewed the armorer.

 You can see behind-the-scenes clips of the scene, including an interview with the armorer, on YouTube at : *Making of Breaking Bad Episode 513.*

It's a 4-minute video covering the gunfight. Pause the clip at 1:39 and you'll see a camera with no one attending it.

The camera operator rolled the camera and walked away, leaving the potential danger zone.

Breaking News : Yesterday the judge in the Baldwin case dismissed the charges due to unprofessional actions by the prosecuting team.

One issue raised in the case was whether an actor has responsibility for checking the safety of a firearm. It's an issue worth discussing but the discussion MUST start with the acknowledgment that the industry has 'best practices' policies that ensure the safe handling of firearms by actors. The armorer and the assistant director have clear directives regarding firearm safety, and they work. On smaller productions without an armorer, the props department assumes the same responsibility and practices.

Bonanza Creek Movie Ranch

Long before the *Rust* production, the Bonanza Creek Movie Ranch was opened for shooting feature films, TV shows, and commercials. First featured in 1955's *The Man From Laramie*, the ranch has been host to *3:10 to Yuma*, *Walker, Texas Ranger*, *Lonesome Dove*, *Silverado*, *Wild Hogs* and *Astronaut Farmer*, to name a few.

The first feature built on the ranch is Daisy Town, a small-scale, old west town built for the joint Italian/German production of *Lucky Luke*, a live-action interpretation of a comic book series popular in Europe. Prior to *Lucky Luke*, there was only one building on the ranch, the McKitrich house, for scenes in *Silverado*. Prior to that, the ranch was simply used as a high desert location – a lone cowboy riding towards the sunset.

As time went on, various productions added buildings to the town plus a cavalry fort and a gold miner's cave entrance. For *Astronaut Farmer* a farmhouse built for *Lucky Luke* was repurposed as the family home of Billy Bob Thornton, Virginia Madsen, grandad Bruce Dern and their kids.

Billy Bob played an astronaut who never got to space. A barn was added next to the house where he built his rocket.

I was unit manager on *Lucky Luke* when the house was built but it was an empty shell, only used for exteriors like scenes on the wrap-around porch. *Astronaut Farmer* fleshed out the interior for their production. The house was built on the edge of a pond with a giant Cottonwood tree hanging over the water. I spent many evenings after wrap sipping a beer on that porch and watching the sunset.

Eave's Ranch

Just up the road from Bonanza Creek is the Eave's Movie Ranch. It was the first 'false front' western town built for film production near Santa Fe. The town was built for *The Cheyenne Social Club* in 1969 featuring Jimmy

Stewart, Henry Fonda, and Shirley Jones and directed by Gene Kelly. The production was lured by tax incentives for filming passed by Governor 'Handsome Dave' Cargo. They were the first tax rebates in the country. Many states now compete for film business with varied rebate rates. That's how New Mexico got *Breaking Bad*.

The term 'false front' refers to buildings that are just a front wall with doors and windows and nothing else, propped up from behind for safety. Every western film set starts with an intersection joining two streets, a saloon, a jail, a blacksmith shop, a hotel, and stables. All of those have built-out, completed, interiors dressed for filming. Other false storefronts are re-decorated and dressed out to add working shop interiors as the script requires.

Each production adds to the set, spending their budget while improving the look of the town for future productions, and the town's owner.

Eaves Ranch was a great western town in its day, but modern life encroached on the edges of the property making it impossible to shoot down a street without seeing a modern home. Hey, it's Santa Fe and home sites are valuable. The town is still a great tourist attraction.

On Set with Dad

I served as Unit Manager on *The Fight Before Christmas*, a joint German/Italian production for the European market. Unit Manager was a position unique to European productions. It was like an on-set production coordinator, a set of eyes and ears on set, reporting to the producer.

Prior to filming I was tasked with finding a trailer for Italian actor Bud Spencer. Bud is a big man, like Andre the Giant. His character always knocks men out with a silly bonk on the head. This was before the internet, so I had to take polaroids of potential trailers and FedEx them to Bud in Italy. Bud approved a trailer and I booked it. But when he got to New Mexico he decided that he needed a bigger unit.

Yikes, I'd already contracted for a great trailer for him, paying up front for a twelve-week rental. What to do ? First, I booked a bigger trailer for Bud. Then I had the first trailer delivered to our set at the Eaves Movie Ranch south of Santa Fe and moved in with my boys. For two weeks we stayed there, parked at the edge of an old false front western town.

After wrap each night the boys would explore the town, carrying a walkie so I could keep track of them. It was great sitting on the steps of the saloon in the empty town as the sun set, chatting with the security guard and radioing the boys : "Miles, what's your 20 ?" – "We're at the jail, Dad."

The security guard was an amazing flautist, playing into the dark night to keep himself company. He, too, had a famed past. He recorded an album in the UK with Phil Collins as his drummer.

Lunch With a Cultural Icon

Work in the film industry led to friendships with lots of politicians and business leaders. During the push for increased tax incentives for the industry, I became fast friends with NM State Senator Shannon Robinson.

Shannon called me one day and invited me to lunch with him and Sister Helen Prejean. Sister Helen was a staunch opponent of the death penalty. Her activism was indemnified in the feature film *Dead Man Walking* starring Sean Penn as a death row inmate. Susan Sarandon won the Best Actress Oscar for her portrayal of Sister Helen.

I was against the death penalty in most cases but made an exception for killers when there was solid evidence, like Ted Bundy. But Sister Helen turned me around, explaining that there was no need to execute killers as they were held in secure prisons and no threat to society. She got to me.

I agree with her.

The Good Life

The Colors of My Life

I think it was the colors of my life that saved me, that kept me engaged.

I painted my house in vibrant colors : a gold room, a red room, a green room, a blue and yellow kitchen. When I worked on *Sparks* with Victoria Principal, I was 38 and wore lots of colorful clothes. One day, when her husband visited our set, Victoria introduced me, saying "This is Charlie, he didn't know what color to wear so he wore them all." That exhortation has guided my wardrobe ever since.

In the Broadway musical *Barnum*, PT Barnum and his wife, Charity, sing dueling lyrics on the song "The Colors of My Life." PT sings of the bright shining colors that attract and vitalize him while Charity bemoans her fate, married to a man who 'wants to give the whole world a paint job' and longing for sage and brown, the colors of the earth.

The colors of my life
are bountiful and bold
the purple glow of indigo
the gleam of green and gold.
The splendor of a sunrise
the dazzle of a flame
the glory of a rainbow
I'd put 'em all to shame.

And the song ends with hope :

And should this sunlit world
grow dark one day
the colors of my life
will leave a shining light
to show the way.

For nearly forty years, when not working, I was pretty isolated. Lots of time spent wasted, watching endless streams of YouTube videos that meant nothing to me. Wasted time. Wasted again.

But ANY film set, production office or location scout was new and filled with discovery. New people, new places, and new situations every day. If you're paying attention, there's no time to be bored.

* * *

Working in entertainment has little perks that vitalize and memorialize the experience. Today, an appliance repairman working on our refrigerator asked for a towel in case the water line leaked. His helper reached for a red and gold beach towel parked on a counter nearby, but I stopped him because that towel held a family memory.

It was the red and gold concert swag beach towel sent to my boys by Shogo Hamada, the Japanese Rock Star from decades ago.

Collecting mementos from productions past keeps the memories of those experiences alive : Our oak dining room set was from the film *City Slickers*, Marshall Dillon's Sheriff's badge from *Gunsmoke: The Long Ride* worn on my *Young Guns II* jacket, and little bags of fake blue meth from *Breaking Bad* – memories of decades well spent.

* * *

Keaton secured permission from the Japanese government to travel to Iwo Jima with a handful of Marines. With permission, he scooped up black sand from the beach where over 6,000 Marines died in battle. A Marine combat photographer captured the moment against the backdrop of Mount Suribachi, made immortal in the photo of Marines raising the flag over the Island. Photo by Sgt. Aaron Patterson, USMC Combat Photographer

Keaton Is My Rock !

Moving to Virginia Beach to join my son, Keaton, and his son, Ossian (ah-shin), has been a lifesaver. Keaton is blessed with a kind heart and limitless patience. And that's a good look for a six-foot-six Staff Sergeant in the United States Marines.

He often claims that it was my patient support that led him to better life choices and to his career in the military. I blush when he gives me credit. He's in his ninth year, serving in Intelligence.

As I mentioned earlier, the lingering effects of TBI are discounted by most people, including MDs, unless they're accompanied by physical deformities. As Neurologist Dr. Meintz said, the prevailing attitude is, 'You look fine, what's wrong with you?' That attitude led to a lot of frustration with friends and colleagues who tried to help me with technology but mistook my inability to grasp whatever they were sharing with a lack of effort on my part.

Living with Keaton has been central to my recovery. For decades I had struggled with technology, unable to use my cell phone for anything other than a simple call. I couldn't even text. And a computer was only a typewriter. The Neurologists in Albuquerque told me that one of the leading issues that I was facing was an inability to sequence. Technology is entirely based on following sequences of prompts. It was difficult. Colleagues at CNM had tried to help me but they'd get frustrated by my inability to grasp their suggestions after multiple attempts. Keaton changed that. His patience has been unlimited, even after walking me through a task a dozen times. He sticks with me until I get it, then helps me again when I forget it.

You may have heard the phrase 'the child is father to the man.' The rock group Blood, Sweat and Tears used the phrase as the title of their debut album. And it's the reality in our household. Keaton carries an air of responsibility, letting me know at all times that he has my back. It's comforting. Saving Grace !

Breaking News : Keaton's in a new assignment in the DC region. Still working in military intelligence, he's been kicked upstairs to play with the big boys in the three letter agencies : FBI, CIA, DIA, plus Homeland Security and the Space Command. He can't tell me any more than that.

You know the line : "If I told you I'd have to kill you."

Monkey Boy – my bestest friend.

Monkey Boy – The love of my life !

I'm blessed to live with Keaton and his son Ossian (ah-shin). Ossian is the love of my life. I call him Monkey Boy. And he returns the favor, enticing me to chase him, calling me 'old man.' He's a paragon of unconditional love !

I moved from my home in New Mexico to live with Keaton when I realized that he was heading for divorce. For decades I'd been a single parent with a demanding career; it's a hard road. It sucked being constantly faced with impossible choices but needing to choose, anyway. My parents in Philly saw my struggles and often said that they wished that they could be there to help. I didn't want Keaton to go through that. I was nearing retirement and without a mate, so I quit teaching, sold my house, gave away most of my belongings, and moved to Virginia Beach. Keaton is a Staff Sergeant in the Marines, a very demanding career. I needed to help. I didn't realize that, once again, my life would be changed.

I moved in a month after Ossian's first birthday. We've been best friends ever since. He's 4 now, rambunctious and smart. Now he calls ME Monkey Boy ! He forces me to live in the moment, a goal of many spiritual paths. No matter my agenda, he will take me by the finger and ask me to play with him. How can I refuse ?

We roll balls in the hall, build imaginary hospitals with wooden blocks, the hospitals are for treating broken cars, and play endless games of tag and hide and seek. Ossian often declares that he's a doctor – sometimes a car doctor, sometimes a people doctor. He loves to run to the freezer for an ice pack that cures all injuries.

Our neighborhood is full of kids who play on our dead-end street, riding bikes, running RC cars, and running around. There are lots of great parks nearby with jungle gyms for kids and a huge playground for them on the beach just ten minutes away. Watching him play and learn how to socialize is a kick.

When Ossian was one, I told Keaton that I intended to support him in music education. I bought him a piano for his second birthday and am planning for him to start lessons when he's five. We sit at his piano occasionally, playing games with the notes, sometimes banging on the keys. At some point he scribbled on the keys with crayons but that will wash off. I followed with a tambourine, a pan flute and some percussion toys.

Early on I introduced him to music videos. He'd sit on my lap and watch musicians from Stevie Wonder to Aretha Franklin and Bruce. But his hands down favorite was a cover of Kool and the Gang's "Celebration" produced by *Playing For Change | Songs Around The World.*

The video starts with boys and girls clapping rhythmically and flows into kids from around the world, playing every instrument you can think of. A boy in the USA starts with a guitar followed by a kid in Argentina on trombone. It goes on from there, drums, keyboards. A cello and violins are joined by an African Children's choir from Uganda, dancing and singing the chorus. All I had to do was start the music and Ossian would run to watch, sitting on my lap. At first he wanted to identify the instruments, pointing at the screen and asking "What dat ?" A few months ago he jumped off my lap and returned with two tambourines for us to join in. The coup de gras came soon after. He still asked "what dat" but he upped the game, turning to me and declaring "me no have" regarding EVERY instrument, sneakily asking to be outfitted like an orchestra. Smart kid.

And he's incredibly industrious. Whenever I cook him breakfast he helps me scramble the eggs and stir the pancake batter. Keaton bought him a plastic toolbox complete with hammer, saw, screwdriver and drill.

Whenever we settle into a home improvement project, he gathers his tools and shows up to help. For quite a while his two favorite phrases were "me do" and "me hep" (help). He's since graduated to announcing, proudly "I did it by myself."

Saving Grace

My last two years in Albuquerque were stressful. I tried to pull my son, Miles, back from the brink and he resented the help. He was too drenched in alcohol and depression to see through to anything else. He didn't have anything uplifting in his life to mitigate the pain. He tried singing karaoke, but karaoke is practiced in bars, so he was always drunk with friends of like mind. He worked regularly but in jobs well below his intelligence level and education. Not very satisfying. I believe that solidified his low opinion of himself. I wanted to help him, but he rejected the help, and it was hurting me. He chose not to speak to me in his final two years.

My grandson, Ossian, was born Feb 29th in Hawaii. The pandemic was raging so I couldn't fly to meet him. Keaton texted me lots of photos, holding Ossian on the beach, cuddling with him as he slept, coaxing him to laugh. But Ossian's mom, Amber, was absent from the pictures. It didn't take long to see that his marriage was in trouble.

Within a year the Marines moved him to Virginia Beach to work as an intelligence instructor. Amber moved with him, sharing a household while they searched for a way forward. Once Keaton declared that they would divorce, I retired from teaching, sold my house, and moved to live with them. I arrived a few weeks after Ossian's first birthday. Divorce was imminent and I wanted to be there to help. Keaton's work was very demanding and I was concerned that Amber might use his career against him to secure custody of the baby, even possibly asking permission to move back to Albuquerque near her family, with Ossian in tow. I figured that my presence in Keaton's home, retired and available to care for Ossian, would render the issue moot. In fact, the result is that I'm the go-to adult, ready to care for him whenever Amber or Keaton need their time for work or whatever. I've been his sole babysitter for three years.

I know it was hard for Amber to put up with me living in her home, but she endured and we're now good friends. She chose to stay in Virginia Beach for Ossian's sake and bought a home just two blocks away, making shared custody relatively easy. It's hard on Amber's mom, Janet, but she comes to visit often for a few weeks at a time, bonding with her daughter and grandson. Janet is a captain of industry, a great role model for Amber and Keaton.

Thanks, Amber and Keaton, for realizing that Ossian is the priority.

* * *

Looking back, I thank God for so many friends and colleagues who stuck with me even though my mental confusion and drug habit was obvious. Thanks to Dave Roberts, Barry Kirk, Kylene Wing and Ann Lerner for your support for ten years at Southwest Productions. Thanks to Randy McComas, business partner, editor and friend of 45 years, for filling in the blanks when I couldn't. Thanks to Stew Lyons for supporting and trusting me. Working with him on *Breaking Bad* and *Better Call Saul* saved me from my crashing self-image. And thanks to my parents. My mom instilled in me a sense of humor and a love of music, my dad taught me responsibility and grace.

I'm still here, and I'm not "dancin' with the doorknob" anymore.

Finis.

Appendix

Abbreviations

AD – Assistant Director – 1st AD, 2nd AD, 2nd 2nd AD

APD – Albuquerque Police Dept.

BLM – Bureau of Land Management

B-roll – shots without dialogue

CNM – Central New Mexico Community College

DP – Director of Photography

HBCU – Historically Black College or University

Jib arm – a crane for extending the reach of the camera

OMI – Office of Medical Investigators

PA – Production Assistant, Pack Animal

PIO – Public Information Officer

POV – Point of View

UNM – University of New Mexico

UPM – Unit Production Manager

Notes

The Band – Yes, there was a band simply named "The Band". They started as the backup band for Bob Dylan and went on to stardom on their own. Their final concert was filmed by Martin Scorcese called *The Last Waltz* featuring the many musicians they backed including Dylan, Eric Clapton, Neil Diamond, Joni Mitchell, Dr. John and Screamin' Jay Hawkins.

Lennie Briscoe was a character on *Law and Order* played by Jerry Orbach for twelve seasons. Jerry also played 'Baby's' dad in *Dirty Dancin'*. He was a Broadway star, appearing in *Chicago* directed by Bob Fosse, and in the original off-Broadway production of *The Fantasticks*, being the first performer to sing the show's standard "Try To Remember."

Ruth Buzzi is best known for her purse-swinging old lady on *Laugh-In*. She's a hoot

Selma Diamond was a character actress with a gruff voice, best remembered as the feisty court clerk in the TV show *Night Court*. She played Steve Martin's opinionated secretary in *All of Me*.

Hector Elizondo – A well-known character actor, he played the hotel manager in *Pretty Woman* who first confronts, then helps a nervous Julia Roberts.

Bob Hartung – Dr. Robert Hartung (Daddy Bob) was my mentor at UNM. He was a producer on the original *Hallmark Hall of Fame* and wrote many of the series' screenplays, adapting the works of Shakespeare and Noel Coward among others. He was nominated for three Primetime Emmy's and four Writer's Guild Awards. He will forever be in my heart.

Leslie Nielsen is best known for his roles in the comedy *Airplane* and for his character Lt. Frank Drebin in *The Naked Gun* films.

Irby Smith – I worked with Irby on *Young Guns II* and *City Slickers*. He was also the 1st AD on *One Flew Over The Cuckoo's Nest* and *Stand By Me*. Irby's son, Jay, married Shannon Kesey, daughter of Ken Kesey, the writer responsible for *One Flew Over The Cuckoo's Nest*. They both worked on *City Slickers*. Jay was on the AD crew and Shannon worked with me as an office assistant.

M. Emmett Walsh – You'd know him if you see him – IMDB lists 232 TV and film credits including the Coen Brothers' *Blood Simple* and *Raising Arizona*.

Fun Filmmaking Facts

* Always cast twins – When young kids and infants are cast in a shoot we usually cast identical twins. That way you can use one while their twin naps or whigs out.

I did a shoot in LA for a kid's medical product. The scene was set in a doctor's waiting room with two moms, a set of twins and a single boy. So we cast identical twins for the single boy and identical triplets for the twins. Yikes, thanks, casting !

Cover set – An indoor set prepared for a last-minute change in schedule due to weather.

Camera department – Starting with the camera operator and supported by AC's, camera assistants. When using film stock there's a 'loader' responsible for loading fresh magazines and preparing shot footage for delivery to the lab. The job of the loader was complicated by the varied film stocks used for specific 'looks.' With digital cameras, the loader is replaced by the DIT – digital imaging technician, responsible for downloading camera cards and supplying empty cards to the cameras.

DP – The director of photography is responsible for the 'look' of the picture, leading the electricians and camera department.

* Garson Studios – The Garson Studios are basketball courts re-purposed as film studios. The classic film star, Greer Garson, paid for the renovation on what was then the College of Santa Fe campus. They were the first studios in New Mexico and *City Slickers* was the first film shot there.

Greens crew – If you stay for the credits on most films you'll find greens men listed. The greens crew supplies large and small plants on set and keeps an inventory of bushes and other live plants to obscure whatever the DP needs camouflaged. They also brush out footprints and tire tracks on sand, dirt roads and snow.

Grips and electricians – Also in the credits you'll see terms that go unexplained. Grips and electricians support each other in lighting a set. The grips supply stands and other supports for lights, like scaffolding, and the electricians supply the lights. Grips also supply the dolly and dolly tracks, and build platforms to support the camera.

> Gaffer – the lead electrician
> Key grip – the head of the grips
> Best boys – second hammer in grips and electricians

Production zone – The production zone is a thirty-mile radius from the production office. Locations within the zone are treated as local but anything outside the zone requires additional pay for travel or hotel accommodations according to union rules.

Teamsters – The logo for the Teamsters Union is a well-known emblem. Most people recognize it but are unsure of the story behind it. There are two horse heads sitting atop a wheel. The horses' names are Thunder and Lightning. Thunder is male, Lightning female. Together, they symbolically represent the pillars of the Teamsters organization: quality and power, dignity and justice, strength and morality. Plus, the Teamsters Union was originally formed when they drove horses pulling wagons. The transpo department is responsible for the trucks that move the company and for all cars seen on-screen in the production, picture cars.

Transpo Dept. – The transportation department is responsible for all vehicle transportation on the set, whether at a studio or on location. That includes forty-foot semi-trailers, cast trailers, and other large trucks to move equipment. The grip and electric departments each require 40' trailers to store and transport their gear. Wardrobe and props also require 40' trailers to house the costumes and props gathered for the run of the show and needed on location.

* TV Pilot – Every year producers shoot pilot episodes, a first episode revealing the concept and cast, hoping to get the green light to continue with the series. Pilot season starts at the end of January and runs through April or May when your series is either picked up or scrapped. When a series gets a green light the exhibitor orders a certain number of episodes and agrees to pay for them.

Video village is a place on set away from the action, where large monitors are set up for viewing by various crew members, mainly the producer(s), the script supervisor, the director, the DP, and VIP set visitors. On outdoor locations, video village is in a tent.

About the Author

Charlie O'Dowd is an entertainer : Actor, singer, director, filmmaker, college professor and author. He served on the management teams of numerous feature films including *City Slickers, Young Guns II* and *Suspect Zero,* topping off his film career on the hit TV series *Breaking Bad.*

He worked as 1st Assistant Director on over 300 national commercials, co-produced two Super Bowl commercials, was a floor director for *ESPN Sports,* a segment field producer for NBC, CBS, ABC, *Entertainment Tonight* and *America's Most Wanted,* and is an award-winning audiobook narrator, having narrated 70 novels and the Bible.

Charlie is retired and lives with his son, USMC Staff Sergeant Keaton Johnson O'Dowd and his grandson, Ossian (ah-shin). Truly two and a half men.

Visit the author online at charlieodowd.com.